Da
pu

Boc
nu

Ple
ano

By the same author

The Economic Pattern
of Modern Germany

NORMAN J. G. POUNDS

Chairman of the Department of Geography
at Indiana University

John Murray

FIFTY ALBEMARLE STREET LONDON

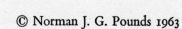

Contents

Preface

The author wishes to express his deep gratitude to all who have helped in the writing of this small book. His thanks are especially due to Professor Emil Meynen and his colleagues of the Institut für Landeskunde, in Bonn; to officials of the West German Foreign Ministry, and to Mrs Susan S. Ball and Miss Joan Atkinson for their assistance in preparing the manuscript and seeing it through the press.

Bloomington, Indiana   NORMAN J. G. POUNDS
   February 1963

Acknowledgments

Thanks are due to the following who have kindly permitted the reproduction of copyright photographs:

Aerofilms & Aero Pictorial Ltd (*Plate 4*); German Information Center, New York (2, 17, 22, 26, 27).

Illustrations

MAPS

Germany Divided

On the eve of the Second World War, in 1937, Germany was one of the largest European countries in both area and population. West of the Soviet Union, her territory was exceeded only by France and Spain, and in population Germany had for many decades been the biggest. It was a highly industrialized state. It stood first on the continent of Europe in the production of coal, iron and steel and of many products of the chemical industries. It was among the foremost manufacturers of textiles and a leader in the fields of fine printing and precision instrument manufacture. Germany possessed a balance between agriculture and industry that Great Britain had long since lost. This is not to suggest that Germany was, or could ever be, self-sufficing; only that the degree of dependence upon imported foodstuffs was relatively small for a country with Germany's degree of concentration on manufacturing industries.

Germany had come late into the industrial field. As late as the middle years of the nineteenth century much of the manufacturing industry was carried on by craftsmen in small workshops, according to traditional patterns and by traditional methods. Then, after the completion of the Zollverein, or Customs Union, and the creation in 1871 of the German Empire, an industrial revolution overtook the country. A remarkable feature of this industrial revolution was that, unlike the experience of Great Britain and of Belgium and to some extent also of France, it was preceded rather than followed by the creation of a net of railway lines. A consequence of this fact was that even at the outset coal and raw materials could be hauled long distances; there was no need for manufacturing to crowd on to the coalfields, as it had done in Great Britain and Belgium, producing dark concentrations of factories and workers' housing. The Ruhr and Upper Silesian industrial regions provide exceptions to this generalization, but most of Germany's industries established themselves in the small towns, from Bavaria in the south to the North and Baltic Seas, from Aachen to Breslau. This was made possible only by a system of transport that was already developed and waiting for industry to use it. For the same reason, the developing urban and industrial centres were able to rely upon distant sources of food for their workers. The dependence of the industries of West Germany on the foodstuffs produced on the great estates of the East (see Chapter 3) has often been exaggerated, but there nevertheless was an interdependence of regions that gave to Germany a functional unity, rare among the countries of Europe. German geographers had some excuse for describing their state as an organism. Each region had become so dependent upon the others that none, it might have been said, could continue to live and prosper in isolation.

Such was the Germany that was invaded from both west and east in 1944 and 1945, and reduced by bombing and gunfire to ruins. When in May 1945 the noise of battle was at last stilled in Germany, this network of intercommunication, this structure of farm and factory, had locally been entirely destroyed and everywhere severely damaged and dislocated. Furthermore, the plans had already been laid for division and occupation of the territory. On the day war ended, it was said, in the area which subsequently became the British Zone, only 10 per cent of the railway track was open; the canals were closed and most of the road bridges destroyed; in the coal mines of the Ruhr only 6 per cent of the complement of miners was at work. Everywhere, factories were destroyed by bombing; power-lines were severed, and water-supplies cut off. There was no government in effective control, and the only movement was of the military transport of the invading armies and the slower and less purposeful creep of the refugees, as they spread westwards from Soviet-occupied areas of Central and Eastern Europe.

On the Allied side plans to partition, to pastoralize and to re-educate Germany had followed one another in quick succession. When the fighting ceased, agreement had already been reached on a division of Germany within her boundaries of 1937. Poland, it had been decided, should receive compensation from Germany for territories absorbed by the Soviet Union. It remained only for the Potsdam Conference (July 1945) to determine the provisional extent of this territorial compensation.

A temporary boundary line was drawn from the border of Czechoslovakia to the Baltic Sea along the rivers Neisse and Oder, but extending west of the Oder, near its mouth to include the city of Stettin on the Polish side of the line. This arrangement was intended to be a temporary one; it was to last only until a peace conference should meet and a definitive treaty of peace between the Allied Powers and Germany be signed. Legally, therefore, the territories east of this boundary are temporarily under Polish and Soviet administration. Nevertheless the countries of the Communist Bloc have recognized these lands as permanently and legally incorporated either into Poland or into the Soviet Union.

The rest of Germany, about three-quarters of the pre-war area within the boundaries of 1937, was divided into zones of occupation (Figure 1). At first three zones were established, British, American and Soviet, and then, in deference to the claims of France, a fourth zone was established in south-west Germany at the expense of the British and American. Again, these divisions were viewed as only temporary, and a re-united Germany, purged of the Nazi philosophy and devoted to the cause of peace, was foreseen for the not too distant future. In the meanwhile, the fiction of the economic unity of Germany was retained, and rebuilding proceeded on the assumption that within a period of at most a few years there would again be one

Germany. The reality proved to be different. During the months immediately following the end of the war, differences and disagreements became apparent between the occupying powers. It proved to be impossible to secure agreement between the Western powers and the Russians on matters of economic policy, or even on the movement of essential goods between the eastern zone and the rest of the country. It was clear that unless the three western zones were able to pool their resources, each was going to become a serious burden upon its occupying power. A start was made in the autumn of 1946 with an agreement between the British and American authorities to bring about an economic fusion of their two zones (the Bizone). The French were more reluctant. Their zone was adjacent to France, and was in certain respects complementary to the economy of France itself. But the increasing tensions between the West and the Russians, coupled with the manifest advantages of the economic fusion of the three western zones, finally overcame the lingering reluctance of France.

In April, 1948, a conference was held in London of the heads of the Allied governments. Later the governmental structure of the future West Germany was discussed with representatives of German authorities, and in the following summer, the Basic Law of the Federal Republic of Germany was drafted. At the same time an Occupation Statute, limiting the rights and obligations of the occupying powers, was prepared and came into effect, along with the Basic Law, in September 1949. Between 1949 and 1955 the restrictive clauses of the Occupation Statute were gradually whittled away, and in 1955 the Federal Republic became a more completely independent and sovereign state.

Germany, (that is to say, the Germany of 1937) thus assumed its three-fold division: the Federal Republic, the Soviet-occupied Zone, and the area now administered by Poland and the Soviet Union. To many Germans these are respectively West, Middle and East Germany, and these expressions are used in this book because they form a convenient

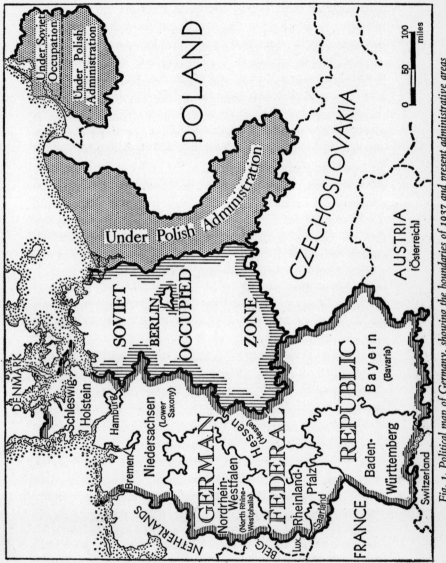

Fig. 1. Political map of Germany, showing the boundaries of 1937 and present administrative areas

way of referring to the parts into which the Germany of 1937 has come to be divided. Their use here has no political significance.★

This process of conferring even greater political freedom and independence on the Federal Republic of Germany was accompanied by an economic revival which, in the words of a British survey of economic conditions, 'challenges comparison with any period in any country in the last 200 years'. The currency reform of June 1948 was the necessary prelude. It endowed the Bizone and later the whole of West Germany with a valid measure of achievement and an acceptable reward for work. It provided an incentive for effort and a reasonable assurance that profits would not be drawn off and lost in an uncontrolled inflation. But the currency reform alone would not have been sufficient, under the conditions existing at this time in Germany, to encourage economic growth and to ensure general well-being. At about the same time that the currency reform was implemented, General Marshall issued his invitation to European states to associate with one another in benefiting from the material aid which the United States was proposing to supply. American aid rescued the West German economy from a dilemma. West Germany lacked the capital for investment in industry, without which the export trade could not be redeveloped and imports of raw materials and foodstuffs paid for. Aid provided under the Marshall Plan provided imports without the immediate obligation of paying for them with exports. At the same time, counterpart funds were made available to the German government, enabling it to invest in agriculture, industry and transport. Above all, the experience of a tremendously successful collaboration with other West European countries was a revealing one to the

★ It should be noted that Middle Germany is often (or usually) referred to in English sources as 'East Germany', while Communist sources use the term 'German Democratic Republic' for this area. Every one of these territorial descriptions is politically 'loaded' in some degree; the author has made his choice on the basis of logic and economy of words, with occasional variations to avoid monotony.

German people, demonstrating that more could be achieved by co-operation than by autarchy and extreme nationalism. The German experience in the Organization for European Economic Co-operation, which arose from the Marshall Plan, led directly to her participation in the Coal and Steel Community, in Euratom, and in the European Common Market.

But this is to advance too quickly in this narrative along the road to German prosperity and equality among the nations. In the dark days of the later 1940's there were two other problems fully as serious as the inflated currency and the lack of capital. These were the Allied attitudes towards German industry and the continued influx of refugees from the East. It is, of course, a truism to say that without heavy industry Germany could not have fought a war. It did not follow that Germany should therefore be deprived of her heavy industry. Various proposals were made on the Allied side during the war for making Germany militarily innocuous after its conclusion. The most extreme of these, associated particularly with the name of Henry Morgenthau, called for the 'pastoralization' of Germany, the reduction of the German people to a nation of 'happy' farmers and shepherds. Germany had too many people and not enough land for so romantic an image ever to have been realizable. The alternative seemed to be to lower the level of German industry to a point at which war—at least, war with all the refinements of modern weapons—would be impossible. Heavy industry, it was decided at Potsdam, was to be reduced to a prescribed level; surplus capacity was to be dismantled and distributed among the Allies, and a level of industry achieved which could support a peaceful people at a level of welfare not above the European average. Furthermore, as the large concentrations of economic power in the possession of the cartels and big concerns were regarded as a factor in Germany's military preparedness, these too were ordered to be broken up. The common ownership of coal-mines and steelworks was ended, and the 'vertical' integration which had characterized the structure of German industry was, formally at least, terminated.

How to fix the level of industry proved to be a more difficult task than had been expected. There was an acute fuel shortage throughout Europe, and in the end no level at all was fixed for the coal industry. The steel industry was thought to be different. The level, which now appears fantastically low, was fixed at 5·8 million tons of steel a year. After the break-up of the quadripartite Control Commission, this figure was raised to 11·1 million tons for West Germany, and iron and steel capacity above what was needed to produce this volume of metal was ordered to be dismantled. It soon became apparent that the policy was ill-conceived and its application ill-considered. Within a short time the Western powers were conniving to raise the level of industry and vying with one another to re-equip the dismantled works. The level of industry was progressively raised, until, with the restoration of complete sovereignty to the Federal Republic of Germany, all attempts at control came to an end.

The other major problem that faced Germany during these difficult early years was that of the refugees. It is convenient to divide these into those who had been forcibly expelled from their homes farther to the east, the *Heimatvertriebenen*, and those who had fled for political reasons. They began to arrive in advance of the Allied armies in 1945, and they continued to come, at a daily average of 500 people, until August 1961, when the Soviet-controlled Middle German régime erected a wall across Berlin and fortified the zonal boundary for all of its 863 miles. Altogether, about 12·5 million have arrived, making up, in a population of about 55 million, almost one person in every four. The largest contingent, about 7 million, came from the lands now under Polish administration. The next largest came from Czechoslovakia. Smaller groups came from the former Baltic States, from Hungary, Romania and the Balkans. Almost all arrived penniless and hungry, and in those dark post-war years each new refugee constituted just one more person to be fed and housed. Now, eighteen years after the end of the war, very few of these refugee families are unemployed. Some may not be doing as well as they had once done farther to the east; very few of the refugee farmers could be employed upon the land in West Germany, but others of the refugees have done very well both for themselves and for their new homeland.

They tended at first to settle just within West Germany's eastern boundary, in an area that had never contained much industry and where the agricultural land was already fully utilized. Many have since filtered westward, especially into the former French Zone of occupation, the *Länder* of Rheinland-Pfalz and Baden-Württemburg. Others have found occupations within the very shadow of the Iron Curtain. The automobile factory of Wolfsburg, where the Volkswagen is made, now employs some 71,000 persons, of whom at least half are expellees from the East. The blossoming industries of Brunswick (Braunschweig) and the iron and steel industry of Salzgitter are now heavily dependent upon the refugee population for their labour supply. Many brought valuable skills from the East, and some of these have set up their own factories or businesses in West Germany. For instance, the German employees of the glass industry of Gablonz, in the Sudetenland, have re-established their old industry at Neugablonz, near Kaufbeuren. It has been said that at least 120,000 businesses have been established by persons who either fled from the Soviet Zone or were expelled from territory now under the administration of Poland, Czechoslovakia or other countries of Eastern Europe. Most of these are light industries—textile and clothing manufacture, glass and ceramics, tool and instrument making. Conspicuous among them, at least to the English consumer, is the photographic equipment turned out, in part at least, by the Zeiss works, re-established at Oberkochen, near Heidenheim, in West Germany.

Fifteen years ago the refugees were a liability. Now the economic expansion of Germany has been able to absorb all, except a small hard-core, into profitable employment. Indeed, a major factor in Germany's economic recovery has been this corps of labour, much of it highly skilled, all of it industrious and eager to make a new start in West Germany.

The prelude to this economic recovery was formed by the Marshall Plan and the currency reform. 'It was . . . this last step which galvanized the economy into a revival which, for pace and volume, challenges comparison with any period in any country in the last 200 years.' In the words of a foreign observer:*

'The black market suddenly disappeared. Shop windows were full of goods; factory chimneys were smoking; and the streets swarmed with lorries. Everywhere the noise of new buildings going up replaced the deathly silence of the ruins. If the state of recovery was a surprise, its swiftness was even more so. In all sectors of economic life it began as the clock struck on the day of currency reform. Only an eye-witness can give an account of the sudden effect which currency reform had on the size of stocks and the wealth of goods on display. Shops filled up with goods from one day to the next; the factories began to work. On the eve of the currency reform the Germans were aimlessly wandering about their towns in search of a few additional items of food. A day later they thought of nothing but producing them. One day apathy was mirrored on their faces while on the next a whole nation looked hopefully into the future.'

In 1949, the Federal Government was established, and a Professor Erhard, who had been in charge of economic affairs since the previous year, now became Minister of Economics. In many ways he was the chief German architect of the new prosperity. His was the decision to minimize governmental control and to allow the freest possible operation of market forces under existing conditions. Nevertheless, support continued to be given to the farmer and to such socially important activities as housing, so that these were not wholly dependent

* Quoted in L. Erhard, *Prosperity Through Competition*, London, 1958, p. 13.

on market forces. It was a *sozialeMarktwirtschaft*, rather than a completely free economy. The tax-structure was manipulated to secure the maximum possible re-investment of profits in capital expansion, and the working of longer hours was encouraged by exempting overtime pay from tax. 'The joy of working', always more real to the German than to the Englishman, 'now meant so much more since wages at last had purchasing power again.' Average hours worked per week increased from 47·2 in 1950 to 49·1 in 1955; they were reduced to 45·6 in August 1960, and have since fallen a little more.

Erhard's policy was to allow the entrepreneur to go where his business instinct led him. Price controls were abandoned, and planning largely discontinued.

The new policy of Erhard led at once to a rise in prices; unemployment, which had hitherto been in part hidden, now appeared to increase. But the greater volume of production soon offset the inflationary tendency and absorbed the unemployed. A moderate devaluation of the D-Mark in September 1949 increased the overseas demand for German products. The Korean crisis of the following summer brought with it a threat to public confidence in this new free-wheeling system. There was for a time a serious balance of payments problem as West Germany's imports temporarily increased faster than her ability to pay for them by means of exports. But soon the pressures of the Korean Crisis increased the demand for coal faster than the mines of the Ruhr were able to satisfy it. The short-lived crisis disappeared, and behind it was left mounting production and productivity, rising real wage-levels and an improving standard of living.

This burst of prosperity is reflected in the growth of West Germany's Gross National Product: the value of all goods and services created or performed during the year. Since 1950, the Gross National Product, expressed in terms of 1954 prices, has more than doubled, and, in terms of actual prices, has trebled:

(Thousand Millions of D-Marks)

1950	97·2	1956	196·4
1951	118·6	1957	213·6
1952	135·6	1958	228·5
1953	145·5	1959	247·9
1954	156·4	1960	276·6
1955	178·3	1961	311 (est.)

(Leistung in Zahlen, Bundesministerium für Wirtschaft, 1961–2.)

It has been argued that too much of this has been ploughed back into capital development, rather than used in expanding consumption. Inevitably, the rate of saving in Germany had to be high, or the ruined cities and industries could never have been rebuilt. That task, however, is nearing its end. Wages have increased much faster than the cost-of-living index, which has risen relatively slowly. The production and sale of consumers' goods has risen very sharply in the past few years, and, despite the high level of taxation and the low level of capitalization of many industries, the outward signs of well-being and prosperity are gradually broadening down from class to class.

West Germany has enjoyed certain important advantages. Until 1955 she did not have to face the burden of maintaining her own armed forces, and since that date her army has been a relatively small one. West Germany was obliged, however, to bear the costs of the military occupation, which may not have been less than those of maintaining an army. On the other hand, she avoided the loss from industry of a significant part of her labour force. The horde of refugees, which at first seemed a serious liability, has been converted into a powerful asset. Secondly, opposition to Erhard's free economy from organized labour has been weak. A strike called in 1948 proved to be ineffective. Since then organized labour has been in some measure associated with management, and has refrained from any large-scale strike action, though it has not always disguised its disapproval of some aspects of a free economy.

Above all the German recovery has been facilitated—one might even go so far as to say it has been made possible—by the

Germans' capacity for hard, continuous, intelligent and disciplined work. Not only have the Germans been willing to work longer hours than were general elsewhere in Western Europe, they have squeezed more into those hours than most other Europeans have been able or willing to do. The result has been the most rapidly growing economy in Europe.

It must not be assumed, from the success which West Germany has achieved despite partition, that the division of Germany was accomplished painlessly. The idea that eastern Germany was agricultural, and western, industrial; that their products were exchanged, and that the interlocking of its parts made Germany an organic whole, has undoubtedly been exaggerated. The severance of the two has not had the disastrous consequences that some gloomy prophets predicted. The fact is that the Lower Rhineland was very far from being the only densely peopled centre of heavy industry; Saxony and Thuringia, now in the Soviet-occupied Zone of Germany, had just as great a proportion of their total population engaged in industry. Parts of the German East, notably East Prussia, Pomerania, and Silesia, were food-surplus areas, but most of this surplus was sent, not to western Germany, but to Berlin and the industrial cities of Silesia and Saxony, or was exported. The present West Germany, i.e. the Federal Republic, in fact, obtained only a small part of its food directly from the territory of the present Soviet-occupied Zone, and the powers which occupied West Germany found that the problems of importing food arose, not from the severance of the Soviet Zone of Germany and the Polish-held territory from the West, but from the influx of refugees. Although the productivity of agriculture has been increased in West Germany, the net food imports of this area are now, in fact, higher than before the war. The reunification of the Federal Republic and the Soviet Zone would provide no solution to the food problem of Germany today, because the population of the Soviet Zone has also been augmented by refugees from the East, and its total agricultural production has in fact declined. The division of West from Middle Germany has not separated an industrially oriented from an agriculturally oriented region. It has, however, separated two industrially developed areas, with different and in some ways complementary industrial systems.

The industrial development of each was in many respects dependent upon its geographical endowment, and that of the Federal Republic will be examined more fully in Chapter 4. Here we can only discuss briefly the nature of the problem. The chief industrial resource of West Germany is its wealth in bituminous coal, especially coal of a quality suitable for the manufacture of metallurgical coke. The Soviet Zone of Germany has immense reserves of lignite, as well as of common salt and potash. West Germany has large, though generally low-grade, reserves of iron ore and possesses the transport facilities which make it relatively easy to import more; East Germany's reserves are small in volume and poor in quality. Industrial development reflected these biases. Iron, steel, and heavy engineering were concentrated in the west. Power generation, chiefly from lignite, was more strongly developed in the east, despite the important Ville region near Cologne (Köln), together with the electro-chemical and electro-technical industries that made heavy demands on power. The manufacture of fertilizers and heavy chemicals, for which the salt and potash deposits were important, was also more characteristic of Middle than of West Germany, as were also the woollen, textile, glass, ceramics, optical, and fine instrument industries, despite the vigorous development of some of these in Württemberg.

In both parts of Germany, excluding the Polish-held territory, post-war development has aimed in part at eliminating these disproportionalities. The Soviet Zone has extended its iron, steel, coking, and oil-refining industries; the Federal Republic, its electric power, heavy chemicals, fertilizers, and light and precision instruments production. This initial disproportion helps to explain the uneven rates of expansion of different sectors of industry in the economics of both the Soviet Zone and the Federal Republic.

2

The Land and the People

The Federal Republic of Germany, with an area of about 95,710 square miles, is little more than half the area even of the Germany that was left in 1919 by the Treaty of Versailles. Yet it is the most varied and in many respects the most valuable part of the former Reich. It contains the Ruhr coalfield and its associated industries, the small but important oilfield of north-west Germany, the great ports of the North Sea coast, and the foci of German history and culture in the Rhineland and South Germany. It contains a very large share of the mineral resources of the earlier Reich, and, though its agricultural potentialities are severely limited in some areas, about 30 per cent of its total area is under crops.

Its territory stretches 530 miles from the Bavarian Alps, which enclose it along part of its southern boundary, to the Danish boundary in Schleswig-Holstein. This is almost as great as the distance from the Isle of Wight, on the south coast of England, to John o' Groats in the north of Scotland. The width of Germany, from west to east, is much less. It is only 270 miles from the French boundary on the Rhine to the Austrian border near Salzburg, and only 140 miles from the Dutch border in the west to the zonal boundary along the river Elbe. The Federal Republic is not a large country. Its area is exceeded by that of France, Spain, Sweden, Finland, Norway, Poland, Italy, and Yugoslavia among the states of Europe.

Yet within this restricted area West Germany possesses a great variety of landscape and resources. It is customary to divide the land itself into physical regions, each characterized by some degree of homogeneity in the contours of its surface.

The southern boundary follows approximately the river Rhine from Basel up to Lake Constance (Bodensee), and from this point eastwards traces out as nearly as is practicable the crest of the Bavarian Alps. West Germany thus contains only about 1,500 square miles of land which may be called alpine. It is a narrow strip, reaching from Lake Constance in the west to the Austrian border at Salzburg in the east. It contains Germany's highest mountain peak, the Zugspitze (9,719 feet) and a number of her most famous mountain resorts, including Garmisch-Partenkirchen and Oberammergau.

North of the Alps and Lake Constance, enclosed between France on the west and Czechoslovakia on the east, and bounded on the north by a belt of higher and less fertile land, is the region which we may call South Germany. This is a varied region in both geological structure and relief. Very broadly, it is built of alternating beds of resistant limestone and sandstone and of softer, more easily eroded clay. These beds have been slightly folded. They are uplifted towards the west and dip gently to the east or south-east. The harder beds form a series of ridges, with steep, scarped slopes facing the west or north-west and gentle slopes dropping towards the east or south-east. The most conspicuous and continuous of these ridges is the Swabian Jura, continued as the Franconian Jura. It stretches from the Rhine in the south-west, diagonally across South Germany to end near Bayreuth against the higher hills which enclose this region on the north. The steep rise of the Swabian and Franconian Jura shuts in the eastern skyline from Stuttgart, Nuremberg (Nürnberg), and Bamberg. Its dry, limestone surface with a short grass, nibbled by sheep, is open and windswept. It is like the Cotswolds, but higher and broader. Very roughly this plateau divides the Danube basin from the Rhine. Down its gentler south-eastern slope small rivers make their way to the Danube, which itself rises near the south-western extremity of the Swabian Jura, or cut back across the escarpment in deeply entrenched valleys to join the Main or Neckar. This region which stretches from the Jura to the Alps

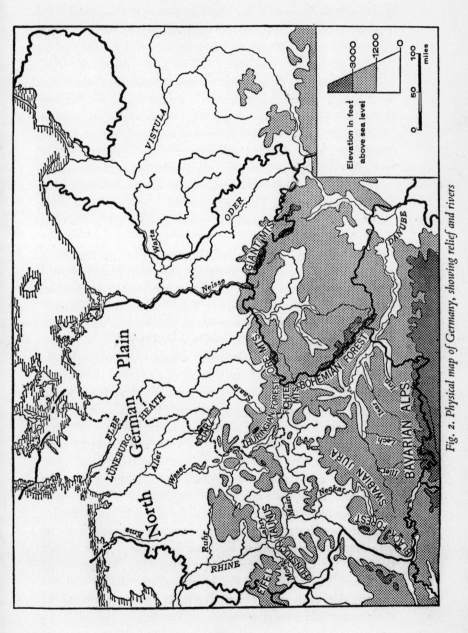

Fig. 2. *Physical map of Germany, showing relief and rivers*

and the Austrian border is a rolling country. During the Ice Age the alpine ice-sheets spread sand and gravel over it. Damp depressions were formed, and have slowly filled with peat to produce the 'moors' of Bavaria. The alpine rivers, the Iller, Lech, Isar, and Inn, flow swiftly northward to the Danube in the shallow valleys which they have etched into the soft and yielding deposits. The monotony of the relief tends to disguise a great variety in the soil: sterile sand and gravel; peat moor; fertile, windblown loess, and here and there the 'solid', the limestones and clays which show through the mantle of later deposits.

The discharge, often violent, of the alpine tributaries has pushed the Danube to the north, forcing it to swing in a great curve towards the Jura and the mountains along the Czechoslovak border. These latter are built of older and harder rocks than the plains and hills of South Germany. They rise steeply to isolated summits and long, forested ridges that have provided a barrier to movement and a deterrent to human settlement. The Bavarian Forest (Bayerischer Wald) overlooks the Danube and is backed by the Bohemian Forest (Böhmer Wald) and the Upper Palatinate Forest (Oberpfälzer Wald).

To the north-west of the Jura, where rocks older in the geological scale than the Jurassic limestone come to the surface, the relief, the soil, and the scenery are more varied. Out in front of the Jura are lesser escarpments, formed by hard beds which occur lower in the geological series: the Löwensteiner Berge, the Frankenhöhe, the Steigerwald, and the Hassberge. The simple pattern of scarp and vale is obscured by the rivers Neckar and Main and their tributaries, which have cut up the ridges and plateaux by a pattern of deep valleys. This region of South Germany was never obscured by the deposits of the Ice Age. Its relief is stronger; the bright colours of the rocks show up along the valleys and in road and rail cuttings. The steeper slopes are forested; the flatter land is cultivated. This region has a richness and beauty in the layout of its villages and the construction of its small towns that make Franconia one of the most scenic and satisfying regions of Europe.

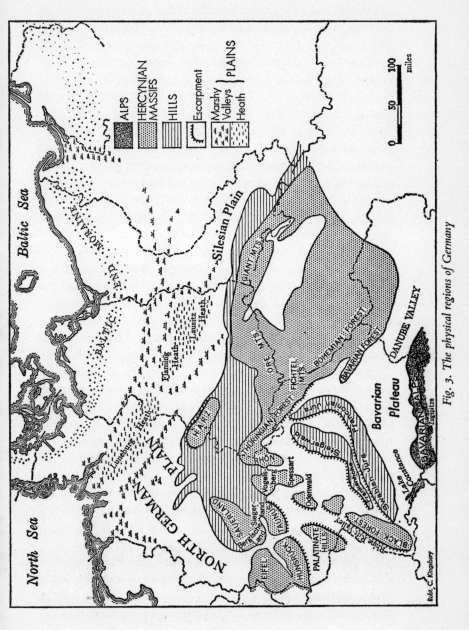

Fig. 3. The physical regions of Germany

The drainage is gathered to the Main and Neckar, which take their winding courses westward to the Rhine. But a physical barrier separates their basins from the river Rhine itself in the form of a ridge of higher and more rugged country. This region begins in the south near Basel, where it towers above the sharp bend in the Rhine, and stretches northward into central Germany, with only a few gaps through which the rivers make their way west to the Rhine. In some ways this ridge resembles the Bohemian Forest. It is built of older and harder rocks than those which surround it; most of it is forested, and it has tended to attract the tourist and repel the farmer. Towards the south, where it culminates in the Feldberg (4,695 feet), it is known as the Black Forest (Schwarzwald), so named from the gloomy spruce forests which cover it. The northern part of the Black Forest ridge is lower, and is separated by the valley of the Neckar, which crosses it between Stuttgart and Heidelberg, from the hills of the Odenwald. These continue beyond the valley of the Main in the Spessart, which in turn runs into the hills of central Germany.

On their eastern side the Black Forest, Odenwald, and Spessart emerge from the rolling hills of Franconia, but along their western margin they end abruptly and steeply against the plain of the river Rhine. Here, between Basel and Mainz, the river Rhine occupies the floor of a rift valley. A section of the earlier crust, about 180 miles from north to south and not generally more than 20 miles wide, has sunk between the Vosges mountains and the Black Forest. River deposits have smoothed out the valley floor, over which the Rhine meanders northwards.

Most of the older settlements lie on the slightly rising ground where the hills meet the river plain: Freiburg, Heidelberg, Darmstadt. Many of the newer lie on the river for the convenience which it affords in transporting freight.

At the northern end of this rift valley, the Rhine valley is shut in by the wall-like massif of the Taunus and Hunsrück. Out in front lies a plain where the Main joins the Rhine and the historic cities of Mainz and Frankfurt have grown up. Around the margins of the plain, between the damp valley floor and the steep forested slopes, are vineyards, and here is Hochheim, which gave us the generic name of Hock wines. At Bingen the wall of rock which lies ahead to the north opens up to reveal a gorge into which the Rhine disappears.

South of the Hunsrück and west of the Rhine is a triangular area of hilly country, remarkably similar in its general features to that which lies beyond the Odenwald to the east. This forms the western part of the Rhenish Palatinate, or Pfalz, a region of rolling hills which passes westwards into the Saarland, the only region of South Germany with significant coal deposits and the only one with an important iron and steel industry.

The third region of Germany is a belt of uplands which extends from the borders of Belgium and Luxemburg on the west to those of Bohemia on the east. The rocks of which it is built resemble those of the Black and Bohemian forests. They are older and harder than the rocks which make up most of South Germany; they are more highly mineralized, and along their northern margin lie the most important coalfields in Europe. Over much of this area these rocks compose a plateau whose undulating surface lies at between one and two thousand feet above sea-level. The rivers have cut deep and narrow valleys across this plateau. Those of the Rhine and its tributary, the Mosel, are so narrow as to form gorges of great scenic value. But to the east, folding and faulting and the erosion of the softer rocks have created large shallow basins within this belt of uplands. These sometimes form good farm country, contrasting with the damp, acid soils and the raw climate of the plateau itself. Along the borders of the Soviet Zone the high plateau reappears, more dissected and broken up into scattered masses than farther to the west: the Vogelsberg and Rhön mountains, the Thuringian Forest (Thüringer Wald) and, lying somewhat detached to the north-east, the Harz mountains, the highest and most famous of all these hill masses of central Germany. The Harz is an abrupt, steep-sided and flat-topped mass of old, hard rock. It is intruded by veins of silver, lead,

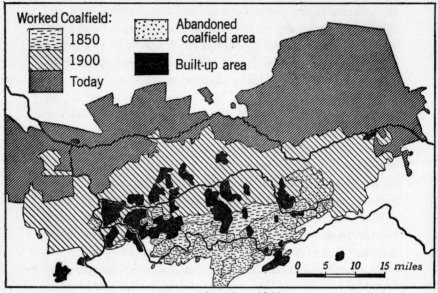

Fig. 4. The Ruhr coalfield

and zinc, and became one of the earliest mining centres in Central Europe. No less famous are its associations with Goethe's *Faust*, with the witches' revelry on *Walpurgisnacht*, and with the travels of Heinrich Heine. The Harz mountains rise abruptly from the northern plain of Germany, but to the

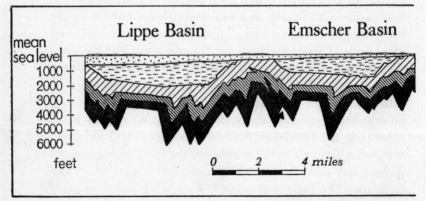

Fig. 5. Geological section

west the hills merge almost imperceptibly into the plain. In fact, the old, hard rocks of which these central uplands are built sink northward beneath the younger rocks of the plain, just as they extend also southwards beneath the scarp and vale of southern Germany. These older rocks have been much denuded as well as intensely folded. Beds of Carboniferous age, which include the coal measures, formerly extended over much if not most of their area. But the coal-bearing rocks have been worn away from the higher surface, and remain, largely obscured and protected by the younger deposits, along the margins.

The Saar coalfield lies against the southern flank of the Hunsrück, but the most extensive deposits lie along the northern margin of these Central German Uplands. Here they form part of a series of coal basins that stretches from northern France, through Belgium and the southern portion of the Netherlands, into Germany, and from Germany eastwards into Poland, Czechoslovakia, and the Soviet Union. Coal is today mined from the small coalfield which lies to the north of Aachen, close to the Dutch boundary, and from several small coal basins in Lower Saxony. But all these are insignificant beside the great resources and the European importance of the Ruhr coalfield.

This coalfield lies mainly to the east of the Rhine, along the

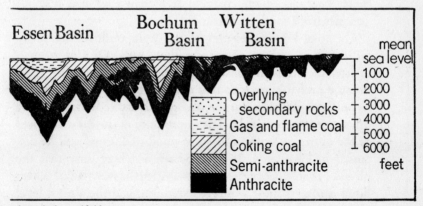

through the coalfield

23

margin of the hill and plain (Figure 4). The coal seams themselves are very numerous, and many are thick enough to be mined very cheaply. They span the whole spectrum of the bituminous coals, from the anthracitic and lean coals at the one extreme to the gas and flame coals at the other. The lowermost, that is the oldest, hardest, and least gassy coals, outcrop within the hills (see Figure 5). Their southward continuation, in a great arch over the plateau of the Sauerland, has long been removed by denudation, but to the north the series, in all its richness and variety, has been preserved by the cover of later rocks. The coalfield extends for at least 70 miles from west to east. Its lowermost beds outcrop along the valley of the little river Ruhr, within the limit of the uplands. Here they have been mined since the Middle Ages. But today the most valuable quality of coal cannot be obtained from this area, and most of the mines along the Ruhr valley have now closed. Higher in the series there occur the most important reserves in the whole of Europe of coking coal. These do not come to the surface, but are buried beneath the later deposits of the northern plain, and can be reached only by deep mines. How far northwards from the southern, exposed margin of the coalfield these beds extend is uncertain. They become gradually deeper until they pass beyond the economic range of mining under present conditions. The area of the coalfield at present exploited is about 30 miles from south to north.

The total known reserves of the Ruhr coalfield are today estimated to exceed 100,000 million tons. Of this from a quarter to a third is considered to be of coking quality. This volume probably exceeds that of the Upper Silesian coalfield, its only close rival in Europe, and greatly exceeds that of every other European coalfield. The importance of the Ruhr coalfield in the economy both of Germany and of Europe will be discussed in Chapter 6. It need be stressed here only that the physical conditions of the Ruhr coalfield, the river Rhine which flows across its most westerly extension, and the almost level plain that stretches northwards to the sea, have facilitated communication and transport, and make it possible to distribute Ruhr coal more widely and more cheaply than that of any other European coalfield.

Somewhat similar to the Ruhr in its location and in its geological conditions is the coalfield of Upper Silesia. It lies, like the Ruhr, on the southern margin of the Great European Plain, and is bordered on the south by the hills of Central Europe. It is larger in area than the Ruhr, though somewhat smaller in its total resources. On it, during the nineteenth century, a great industrial complex was developed (see p. 72), and it early profited, though to a smaller degree than the Ruhr, from the water-borne transport facilities provided by the river Oder. Most of the coalfield and industrial area lay within Germany before 1918. By the Versailles Treaty, about two-thirds of it passed to Poland, and since 1945 the remainder has been under Polish administration.

To the north-west, within the hills which border Lower Silesia, is the Waldenburg (Polish-Wałbrzych) coalfield. It is small in total resources and difficult of access, but derives its industrial importance from the fact that it is able to provide much-needed coking coal for the blast furnaces.

The North German Plain

The belt of uplands that we have just examined is bordered on the north, as it is on the south, by younger and softer rocks. Limestones and sandstones, with intervening beds of soft clay impart a wave-like pattern to the land. Limestone ridges rise like waves about to break against the ancient massifs of the Sauerland and the Harz. But this region of ridge and vale, similar in so many ways to Franconia and Swabia, covers only a small area. It forms a narrow belt, lying from west to east along the margin of the uplands and the plain. It is only a few miles wide, and to the north it dips beneath the deposits, like those which cover southern Bavaria, left by the Ice Age. Yet within this narrow region is found most of Germany's iron ore resources. It is a low-grade ore occurring in thick beds in the limestone. It is highly phosphoric, and its smelting and refining long presented serious technical problems. This ore is widely distributed, but it occurs in workable quantities chiefly along the foreland to the north of the Harz mountains. The existence of these deposits has been known for a long time, and they were occasionally worked before modern technology made it possible to smelt them on a large scale. They now provide most of West Germany's output of iron ore, and supply the smelting works at Salzgitter, near Brunswick, and Peine, near Hanover.

This narrow belt of country, lying between the plateau and the plain, is one of the most fertile and productive regions of Germany. It lay too far to the south and too high above sea-level ever to have been impaired by the sand, gravel, and boulder clay spread by the ice-sheets and by the rivers that flowed from them. Instead, this region received only the fine dust-like loess, carried by the winds and deposited to form a deep, light, well-drained soil. This loess belt was too dry ever to have been densely forested; it attracted early settlement; it provided an early route-way, and is today distinguished by the intensity of its cultivation and the density of the rural and urban settlement that has arisen along it. Today it stretches in an almost continuous belt from the region of Aachen in the west to Silesia in the east.

The plain to the north is distinguished from this region, not by the contours of the surface, but by drainage and soil and the resulting vegetation and land use. The North German Plain, together with its extension west into the Netherlands and east through central and eastern Germany into Poland is a product of the Ice Age. If there had been no Ice Age, much of its area would now be beneath the North or Baltic seas. Four times in the Quaternary period the ice-sheets spread south from Scandinavia; when they melted they left a thick accumulation of clay, sand, gravel, and boulders. Much of this was washed out by meltwater as it flowed from the ice. It was sorted and graded by the action of the water: banks of coarse gravel were formed, merging gradually into finer sands. Elsewhere the heavy, impenetrable clay remains, little altered either by Nature or the hand of man: a damp, heavy soil, difficult to plough and best left under pasture or forest. The margin of the ice-sheet stretched south-eastwards across Central Europe. The water that discharged from it flowed parallel with the ice-margin towards the North Sea, excavating a valley across whatever rocks and deposits lay in its way. The ice-sheet retreated, and these glacial rivers shifted their course to the north-east, only to cut another valley along their new route to the sea. Today the North German Plain is seamed by these parallel valleys. Not all of them now contain water, and where rivers do continue to flow they are small compared with the rivers that must have once gushed from the ice-sheets. The rivers have tended to 'jump' from one valley to the next. The Elbe, for example, instead of continuing the direction of its upper valley towards Bremen, deserted this valley at Magdeburg and skipped over to the next valley which formerly carried the Oder to the sea at Hamburg. The Oder meanwhile skipped to the right to make its way to the Baltic Sea north of Stettin. The result is a network of valleys, some of which are occupied by rivers, while others (called by the Germans *Urstromtäler*) are now abandoned by the primeval glacial rivers which formed them. The latter are damp and marshy; their beds are filled with soft clay; no water flows through them, but they lie ready for the engineer to cut a canal to link up the natural rivers. Thus the Rhine has been linked with the Ems, Weser, and Elbe, and the Elbe is joined to the net of waterways, part natural and part artificial, which encircles Berlin and is continued east to the Oder, the Warthe, and the Vistula.

The North German Plain has thus come to be built around a pattern of criss-cross lines formed by the damp river valleys. Between them, and contrasting with them, are the areas where the glacial deposits have been little disturbed. These intervening areas are made up, on the one hand, of heavy glacial clay which supports the meadows and pastures of Schleswig-Holstein and Westphalia, and, on the other, of the sandy terminal moraines.

These latter form ridges along the lines, roughly from north-west to south-east, where the ice paused temporarily in the course of its retreat. Sand, gravel, and boulders piled up, while the finer material was carried away to the rivers and the sea. Today this coarser material supports heathland, most conspicuously, in the Lüneburg Heath (Lüneburger Heide). In its natural condition this was a large, elongated region, drawn out between the Weser and the Elbe, where the dry, sandy soil resisted the efforts of man to tame and cultivate it, where heath plants grew readily, and the rounded hills were ablaze with purple heather in summer, and the German youth hiked and camped. Patches of this land have been brought under cultivation, but large areas have in recent years been planted with conifers, and constitute one of Germany's most important sources of softwood lumber.

Yet another type of landscape has formed in the period since the end of the Ice Age along the coast of North Germany. Here the vast quantities of silt, washed from the moraines and borne northwards by the rivers, have been deposited to form coastal marshes. These border the estuaries of the rivers, line the coast, and have been growing seaward with the fresh deposits of silt at a relatively rapid rate.

The mineral resources of the northern plain consist of coal and oil. The former, dipping northwards from the margin of the uplands, lies at too great a depth to be mined in the near future. Only locally, as at Ibbenbüren, near Osnabrück, just within the margin of the hills, does it come within distance of the surface. The petroleum is more easily reached, though the development of the Lower Saxon and Schleswig-Holstein oil-fields has occurred only during the last few years. There seems to be a belt of oil-bearing rock deep beneath the surface and extending from the Dutch border in the west to the border of the Soviet Zone of Germany. This reserve is now being tapped, especially in the Ems and Weser valleys.

These physical divisions of Germany lie in a west to east direction, like the warp of a fabric. Through them are threaded the rivers, like the woof, tying the physical regions together. Foremost among these rivers is the Rhine itself. No geographical feature of Germany is more prominent in German history, folk-lore, and legend than this river along whose banks German civilization arose. Yet the Rhine is not wholly a German river. It rises in Switzerland. For over 60 miles it constitutes the boundary between Switzerland and Germany, and for about another 112 miles that between Germany and France (Alsace). Then for about 300 miles it is wholly German, before entering the Netherlands and breaking up into the distributaries which form its delta.

Above Basel the Rhine is not continuously navigable. Stretches of calm, gently flowing river are interrupted by rapids or falls, of which those at Schaffhausen are the most formidable. But at Basel the Rhine makes an abrupt turn to the north and meanders across the generally level plain of the Rift valley. On each side, before the construction of the Rhein-Seitenkanal from Basel to Breisach, were water meadows, and in the distance is seen the blue line of the Vosges and of the Black Forest. The navigation of this section of the river was formerly obstructed by the sharp twists and the rapid changes of its course. The course has been straightened and is today being further improved by the construction of dams and locks which serve the dual purpose of regulating the river's flow and facilitating navigation.

Farther north the Rhine is joined by two of its more important tributaries, the Neckar and the Main. The Neckar rises on the Baar, between the Black Forest and the Swabian Jura, and in its meandering course drains much of the hilly lowland between the Jura and the Black Forest. The Main rises in the Fichtel-Gebirge, the rounded, mountainous boss that lies close to the north-western corner of Czechoslovakia. From here it flows westward by a zigzag course to join the Rhine opposite Mainz. Its chief branch, the Regnitz, flows west from the Franconian Jura, where only a low divide separates its basin from that of the Danube. Both Neckar and Main are navigable for considerable distances, and in recent years man has improved on Nature by building dams and locks and canalizing both rivers. Large barges can ascend the one to above Stuttgart, and small barges the other as far as Bamberg. The old canal which parallels the Regnitz is being rebuilt and will be extended from Nuremberg, through the Jura, to the Danube. In this way most of South Germany will be attracted within the transportational sphere of the Rhine.

Near Mainz the river makes a jog to the left, searching, as it were, for a way through the barrier of hills which confronts it. Then at Bingen it turns sharply to the north and for 75 miles flows across the slate plateau of the Central Uplands. This is the most famous and most scenic section of the Rhine's course between the mountains of Switzerland and the Dutch coast. Yet it is not an easy section of the river to navigate. The river, held between its steep rock walls, is unusually swift, and in earlier times its eddying currents were a grave menace to small ships. The legend of the *Lorelei*, immortalized in Heine's poem, perpetuates the memory of the hazards of one section of this course. The Rhine receives a number of short, swift rivers that descend from the plateau that encloses it, as well as two larger, longer, and more important rivers, the Mosel and the Lahn, which rise in eastern France and the Siegerland respectively. Like the Rhine, they also have cut their gorge-like valleys across the massif of ancient rock.

At its northern end the Rhine gorge ends almost as abruptly as it began. The hills draw back from the river. The serrated volcanic hills of the Siebengebirge droop down towards the north, and the river widens as it advances into the plain. Here there were never any serious obstacles to navigation. The Rhine, with its interminable succession of barges, sweeps past the cities of Bonn, Cologne, Düsseldorf, and Duisburg. It crosses the western extension of the Ruhr coalfield, where it picks up the rivers Ruhr, Emscher, and Lippe and the cargoes of coal and steel from the *Ruhrgebiet*, and then flows on to the north-west and into the Netherlands. The traffic sweeps on to the port of Rotterdam, or diverges through the Dutch canals to Rotterdam or the Belgian port of Antwerp.

No other river has the unifying qualities nor the importance in German economic life of the Rhine. It is one of the most-used navigable rivers in the world. It drains almost two-thirds of the area of the Federal Republic; canals link it across the northern plain with the Ems, Weser, and Elbe, and south-eastwards a canal is being constructed to link it with the Danube.

The previous pages have described the physical variety to be found in Germany. Its regions can be grouped into those which have always been particularly gracious and hospitable to man; where the soil is good and agriculture easy; where transport has been facilitated by navigable rivers, and industry by fuel resources; where cities developed early and population has always been dense; and, on the other hand, into those regions of rugged relief, poor soil, or harsh climate, which have always repelled human settlement and made human life arduous and difficult.

To the former belong the loess belt of the Upper Rhine valley and the borderland of the central hills and northern plain. They include also the plain of Lower Bavaria; several small basins set amid the hills of Central Germany; the valleys of the Neckar and middle Main; and small, fragmentary areas in the northern plain.

To the latter belong the plateaux and hilly ridges which stretch from the Eifel in the west to the Czechoslovak border in the east, with outliers, like the Spessart and the Black Forest to the south. This group includes also the high, raw plateaux of the Swabian and Franconian Jura and of other scarplands in South Germany, and it embraces the sandy heaths and poorly drained clays of the northern plain and, by contrast, the Alps which enclose Germany on the south.

Climate

The Federal Republic of Germany lies in north-western Europe, and is, like its neighbours to the north of the Alps, a land of cool summers and mild winters, and of regular and well-distributed rainfall. But there are considerable variations within Germany, and the day-to-day changes of the weather may depart very widely from the seasonal averages of temperature and rainfall. Western Germany is dominated in turn by maritime air which blows in from the Atlantic Ocean, and continental air that comes from the south-east, east, or northeast. The maritime air is mild and damp. In winter it raises the temperature, and in summer it cools it, and at all seasons it brings rain. The continental winds of summer are hot; those of winter are cold. Exposure to the continental air masses is least in the coastal region of the north-west, and here the seasonal temperature range is the smallest. Emden, for example, at the mouth of the Ems, has a January average of 34°F. and a July average of 62°, a range which differs very little from that of eastern England. With increasing distance from the coast, the winters become more severe, and the summers warmer. The January average at Hanover is 32°; at Frankfurt 31°; and at Munich 28°. These locations are only a short distance above sea-level; at greater altitudes the January temperatures are very much lower, and the winter snow lies long on the plateau surface of the Central Uplands, and in the Black Forest and Bavarian Forest, and longer still in the Alps. Contrariwise, the summers become warmer towards the south and east. The July average rises to 65° in Frankfurt and 67° in the Rift valley farther to the south. The rainfall pattern also changes somewhat with increasing distance from the coast. Near the sea the wettest season is in autumn and winter, as it is over most of the British Isles. But only a short distance inland the volume of summer rainfall begins to increase, and the autumn and winter maximum gradually disappears. The wettest months come to be June, July, and August, and in central Germany this period is found to receive from a third to a half of the annual total. Much of this summer rainfall occurs in storms, sometimes of exceptional violence and frequently accompanied by hail. Much of the smaller winter precipitation comes as snow.

1. The 'Wall', in front of the Brandenburger Tor, is the emblem of Germany's division

2. Hundreds of small cars on the German roads demonstrate the new prosperity of West Germany

3. *The German Baltic Coast; this rather chilly bathing beach is on the shore of the Kiel Fiord*
4. *The heath landscape of the North German Plain*

5. The rolling, wooded hills of the Sauerland. In the foreground is the Agger Dam and lake, used to conserve water for the Ruhr industrial region

6. The hills of Central Germany are broken by lower areas of good farmland. This scene was taken on the edge of the Taunus

7. *A 'street-village'* (Strassendorf): *Konradswaldau in Lower Silesia*
8. *The Mosel valley at Cochem, with its vineyards*

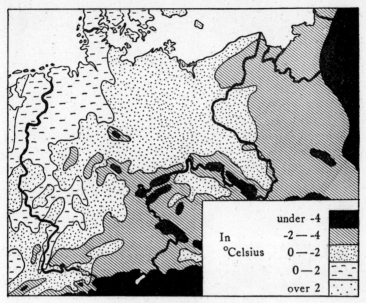

Fig. 6. Temperatures in January

Fig. 7. Temperatures in July

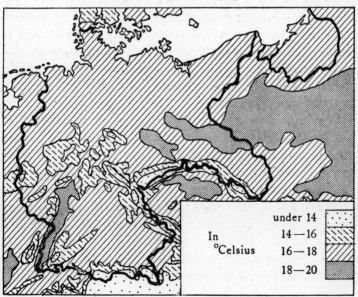

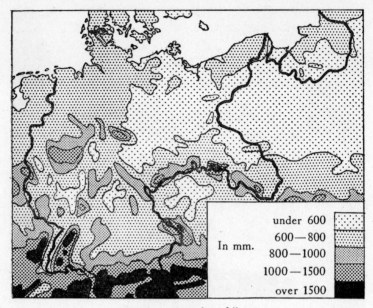

In mm.		
	under 600	
	600—800	
	800—1000	
	1000—1500	
	over 1500	

Fig. 8. Annual rainfall

Snow-cover is intermittent over the lower land, but on the hills it comes in late autumn and may lie with little interruption throughout the winter. The cold is rarely severe enough in western Germany for any thick and lasting ice to form on lakes and rivers. There is little interruption of the navigation of the Rhine, whose swift current freezes less readily than the calm water of lakes and canals.

The behaviour of German rivers reflects the climate of Germany. Little of the small winter precipitation is evaporated into the cool humid air, and most flows by way of the rivers to the sea. In most German rivers the greatest flow is in late winter and early spring, when the soil is wet and can absorb no more, and the snows are melting from the hills. The river level in summer is generally lower; much of the rainfall is evaporated back into the atmosphere, though occasionally flash floods result, especially in hilly areas, from the violent rainstorms. The Rhine is an exception. It derives much of its flow,

34

not from the rain and snow of Germany, but from the melting snow and ice of the Alps. Melting is most vigorous through the summer months, and throughout the upper half of its course the river level is highest and its flow most rapid in summer, but below Mainz the influence of the tributaries which join it from the central German uplands gradually tips the balance from a summer maximum, first to a discharge that is spread evenly through the year, and then, in the river's lowest course, to a winter maximum.

These are the physical conditions under which the Rhine is used. They determine the draft of barges and the power of the tugs. In summer one sees a Rhine tug barely making headway against the swift current, and in winter the barge may be only part loaded so that it will draw less water in the shallow parts of the river.

Soil and vegetation are also in part a response to the climate, but West Germany is too small an area, and the climate over the whole too uniform, for sharp regional variations to be apparent. The soils and the differences in vegetation owe their origin mainly to the changing geological pattern of the rocks and to the irregular deposit of glacial materials. Germany is not a country of high natural fertility; it has little comparable, for example, with the great, *limon*-covered plains of France, or the black-earth steppe of the Ukraine. Good soils occur over small areas, but much of the country has soil which is indifferent if not poor, and which can be made to yield good crops only with a heavy expenditure of fertilizer and labour.

The soils of the northern plain are either too damp to be easily cultivable, or are too acid and sterile to be worth the effort. Reclamation and drainage have added in recent years to the extent of farm-land along the valleys and the coast, but from the dry heathlands, like the Lüneburg Heath, the greatest profit is to be obtained by planting them with softwood trees. Most of the area of the Central Uplands, with its hard rocks, yields only a thin soil, heavily leached by the rainfall. South Germany is a patchwork quilt in the pattern of its soils, as it is

also in that of its geology: heavy soils on the clay; dry, cal-
careous soils on the limestone ridges; sour, sterile soils over the
high ground of the Black Forest, the Odenwald, and the hills
along the Czechoslovak border, and patches of acid peat in the
'moors' which have filled the depressions in the glacial drift of
Bavaria. But between them are the few, small areas of supremely
good soils; the patches of wind-blown loess which are scattered
over the plains of South Germany, which lie along the Rhine
valley from Basel down to Mainz, fill out the Stuttgart basin,
and the middle part of the Main valley and, above all, extend
up in a continuous belt along the border of the Central Uplands
and the northern plain all the way from the Netherlands border
in the west, through central and eastern Germany and into
Poland. This is the loess belt *par excellence*, a region of light,
dry, fertile soil; never heavily wooded, always easily cultivated,
and throughout human history providing an avenue of human
migration and movement.

Natural vegetation and cultivated plants are partially adapted
to both climate and soil. To the ancients Germany was a
forested land. It was the *Silva hercynia*, the region of pathless
forest into which the Romans ventured only occasionally. On
the damp plains of the north there grew oak woodland on the
clay and the more open birchwoods on the sands. Along the
valleys must have grown willow and alder and over large areas
there can only have been a swamp vegetation. The Central
Uplands and the plains and plateaux of South Germany had
characteristically a cover of beechwood, which passed upwards
into spruce and fir forest on the highest ground.

Germany remains today a very well-wooded country, with
no less than about 28 per cent of the area of West Germany
classified as forest. But very little of this is natural forest. The
human migration and settlement, which marked the Middle
Ages, brought about a widespread reduction of the forest. Most
of what we see today is subsequent growth or recent afforesta-
tion. Today the forest covers the steeper slopes of the mountains and uplands and the areas of poor soil which occur in

most parts of Germany. Formerly broad-leaved trees predominated; today coniferous trees make up about 65 per cent of all the forest in the Federal Republic, and an even greater proportion in the Soviet Zone of Germany. The spruce (*Fichte*) alone is said to make up 40 per cent of the forest in the Central Uplands and South Germany, and the pine (*Kiefer*), which is more tolerant of dry, sterile, sandy soils, predominates on the former heathlands of the northern plain.

About two-thirds of the area of West Germany is farm-land. A relatively small proportion of this—only about 55 per cent— is actually crop-land, and most of the remainder is meadow and pasture. This fact springs from the conditions of climate and soil existing in West Germany; much of the land, especially in the northern plain, is too damp and heavy to be cultivated, and the poor soils which cover parts of the Central Uplands are best left under grass. Intensive crop-farming is important only on the areas, rather limited in extent, of medium and good quality soils.

The food-producing capacity of western Germany is thus severely limited. The physical limits of cultivation could unquestionably be expanded as, in fact, they were during the 1930s, when Germany aimed to become more nearly self-sufficing. But this could be achieved only at a high cost in labour, in land reclamation, and in fertilizers. The German people have concluded—and rightly—that their investment is better placed in those branches of industry for which their land offers peculiar advantages, rather than in those for which it is but little suited and which can be carried on only at a high cost. Middle Germany (the Soviet Zone) is very little better suited than West to crop-farming. The vast areas of heath-land greatly reduce the cultivable area, and the longer and more severe winters shorten the growing period. On the other hand, the area of damp, ill-drained soil is less and the diminished winter precipitation makes this an area more suited to crop than to animal farming.

The south-western corner of the Federal Republic combines the advantages of good soil and of a more genial climate than is to be found over most of Germany. This is particularly true of the land bordering Lake Constance (Bodensee) and of the narrow strip of land between the Black Forest and the Rhine, continued northwards into the plains around Mainz and Frankfurt. The dusting of loess ensures a higher fertility than over much of Germany; the protection afforded by the encircling hills gives it more sunshine, and its more southerly latitude leads to an even earlier spring and a longer and hotter summer than in the rest of Germany. In spring the apple orchards are in blossom here a full month before they bloom in the Central Uplands and the northern plain. This is in fact a fruit-growing region, and the best suited in all Germany for this crop. Among other fruits the grape-vine is prominent. It covers the narrow plain and low hills which line the ancient *Bergstrasse*, the ancient road that runs north along the foot of the Odenwald. The vineyards clothe the hills around the Mainz plain and border the so-called *Weinstrasse* which extends southwards to the French border, but this far north they keep to the south-facing slopes to get the maximum insolation from the summer sun. The vineyards extend northwards down the Rhine gorge and up the valleys of the Mosel and Ahr, spread over their sunnier slopes. But near Bonn the climate becomes too cool and cloudy for profitable viticulture, and there the last vineyards give place to apple orchards and vegetable farms to supply the industrial cities.

These are the physical conditions amid which the German people has lived and worked. This is not a harsh or unfavourable environment; nor, on the other hand, is it particularly gracious and easy. The beauty of the German landscape is compounded of elements that individually are by no means helpful to man. The bright, open, breezy heath-land covers as poor a soil as any to be found in Europe; the rolling hills of South Germany are built of dry limestone, the tumbled landscape of the Central Uplands has been carved into hard rock, which breaks down only slowly to form at best an indifferent soil.

Only in its mineral endowment is Germany peculiarly fortunate. The present industrial development of Germany would be inconceivable without its resources in coal, both the bituminous coal of the Ruhr, of the Aachen field, and of the Saarland, and the lignite which occurs most abundantly, as far as the Federal Republic is concerned, near Cologne. Although German deposits of iron ore have been relatively unimportant until recently, newer technological developments are allowing greater use to be made of them. Non-ferrous metals and other minerals, such as potash and common salt, are better represented in the central and eastern parts of Germany than in the west, but West Germany does contain most of Germany's reserves of mineral oil, enough to meet about a quarter of her needs. Though imports of oil must necessarily be large, the Federal Republic fares very much better in this respect than any other West European country.

In the field of transport Germany's advantages are perhaps unique in Europe. Endowed by Nature with rivers unusually well suited, even in their natural condition, for navigation, the German people have succeeded in improving them and in integrating them by a system of canals. Even for the construction of canals, North Germany in particular possessed exceptional advantages in the flat, marshy valleys of former rivers.

THE PEOPLE

The German people have evolved from those Germanic tribes who settled in Central Europe in late prehistoric times and, after the fall of the Roman Empire, filled out the area which has ever since borne their name. In 843 the empire of the Christian West, which had been created by the Emperor Charlemagne, was divided between his heirs. The easternmost division of this Frankish Empire was the nucleus of the later 'Holy Roman Empire of the German Nation'. Within that empire the German kings and emperors of the Middle Ages continued a Christian and imperial tradition. They opened up the whole of Central Europe to their culture; they defended the West against attacks by the Avars, the Magyars, the Mongols, and finally the Turks, and they created an orderly supra-national state.

The German Empire not only opened up to the Christian West wide areas in the east and south-east of Europe, converting to Christianity the Magyars and the Western Slavs, but it also imparted to these peoples a higher culture and civilization, just as the German tribes had themselves absorbed the higher civilization of ancient Rome through the cities and other points of contact along the Rhine and Danube.

The highly developed medieval German city communities and the artistry and craftsmanship of their guilds derives ultimately from the Romano-Celtic civilization of early Rhineland and South German cities, like Cologne, Mainz, Trier, Coblenz, Regensburg, Augsburg, and Constance. These were joined during the Middle Ages by cities of newer foundation: Nuremberg, Ulm, Frankfurt, Magdeburg, Lübeck, and many others. In their trade and commerce and their municipal institutions and organization, they extended their influence and their example eastwards, through Poland, and into the Baltic region and the Danubian basin.

The economic growth both of Germany and of its neighbours was shaped by the leagues of commercial cities which had their centre in Germany. Foremost among these was the Hanseatic League, whose members—prominent among them Hamburg, Cologne, Lübeck, Bruges, London, Bergen, and Danzig—carried their trade far into Russia. The present designation of the English unit of currency, the 'pound sterling', derives from these early commercial relations, and was the name of the coin, the 'Easterling', used in this trade.

In a similar way, the influence of merchant cities in Central and South Germany, such as Frankfurt and Augsburg, and of their merchant families like the Fuggers and the Welsers, reached as far as the Levant. One of their units of currency, the 'Thaler' which was minted at Joachimsthal in Bohemia, has continued until today as the 'dollar'.

In this settlement of Central and Eastern Europe other peoples —the Dutch, Flemings, French, and even English and Irish— participated. It was a slow, eastward advance of peasants and landowners, who cleared forests, drained land, founded cities, and established trade. Thus was the frontier of German settlement advanced first beyond the Elbe and then beyond the Oder.

The present urban pattern of Germany was in large measure established during the Middle Ages. There have since been changes—some of them drastic—in the relative importance of cities, with the expansion of industry. Medieval Berlin was small and insignificant; Munich was overshadowed by near-by Augsburg, and the cities of the Ruhr and Saarland were little more than overgrown villages. The medieval urban pattern remained substantially unaltered until the second half of the nineteenth century. The population of Germany as a whole was growing rapidly at this time, and the expansion of the urban population was especially rapid. A kind of selective process distinguished those cities most favourably sited for modern industry and trade from the others. The former included most of the prominent centres of medieval crafts and trade, which continued to benefit from the simple advantages of their site and situation. It included also cities like Essen, Dortmund, and Saarbrücken, whose rapid growth resulted from the newly discovered wealth of fuel; those such as Düsseldorf, which were centrally placed in rich farming land, and those like Mannheim and Duisburg, whose importance derived from the revived importance of river transport. On the other hand, many a city, prominent or even distinguished in medieval Germany, like Goslar, Rottweil, and Nördlingen, failed to benefit from the new shape of an industrial Germany, and remained small and of mainly local importance. Those factors, however, which inhibited their industrial and commercial growth, served to perpetuate their picturesque and old-world atmosphere, which never fails to attract the tourist.

The fluctuating boundaries of the individual German states

and the political fragmentation of Germany before the last century make it difficult to form a reliable estimate of total population. In 1720 it is estimated that there were between 14 and 15 million living in the area that was to become, a century and a half later, the empire of the German Kaiser. It may have been higher than this before it was reduced by the appalling destruction of life and property which characterized the Thirty Years War and other struggles of the seventeenth century. By 1819 it had risen to about 26 million. On the eve of the First World War it was 67,790,000 and in 1937, after the losses of 1919 and before the incorporation of Austria and parts of Czechoslovakia, it had again reached 67·8 million.

At the end of the Second World War, the territories lying east of the Oder and Neisse were occupied by Poland, with the exception of part of East Prussia, which was annexed by the Soviet Union. Most of their German population either fled before the approach of the Red Army or was later expelled by the Poles, most of it to find refuge in West Germany. The territory of the Federal Republic is now more densely peopled than at any time in the past. Its population in 1960, including that of West Berlin, amounted to 55·6 million. That of the Soviet Zone of Germany, including East Berlin, was put at 17,286,000 in 1960, suggesting a total for all Germany, west of the Oder–Neisse line, of about 72,900,000 in that year.

A century ago the population of Germany was still predominantly rural. The majority lived in villages or in very small towns whose function lay more in farming than trade or the crafts. The urban sector of the population has since grown steadily, and with it the size of the fraction employed in industry. The sharpest increase in the size of the industrially employed population has been during the past decade, with its unprecedented industrial boom. In 1954 over 35 per cent of the population of West Germany was employed in manufacturing industries alone. By contrast with this growth in the industrial sector, agriculture has remained relatively stagnant. To the role of agriculture in the German economy we must now turn.

3

Agriculture

About 14 per cent of the working population of Germany is engaged in agriculture, but the products of farming and forestry contribute only about 6 per cent of the gross national product of Germany. Germany is not primarily an agricultural country, and for over a century a substantial part of all the foodstuffs consumed has had to be imported. The vigorous efforts that were made by the National Socialist Government to make Germany self-sufficing met with failure and left a large gap between domestic production and needs, which had to be bridged by imports. Today about a quarter of total food requirements has to be imported. The eastern provinces of Germany, which were on balance a food-surplus region, have passed under Polish administration, and the Federal Republic has found its population increased by the influx of refugees. On a rough estimate, the food needs of the Federal Republic are today about 30 per cent larger than the needs of the same area before the Second World War.

The alleged complementary nature of western and eastern Germany was a common theme both of German publicists and of western statesmen. Winston Churchill complained that 'as it stands at present the Russian occupational zone has the smallest proportion of people and grows by far the largest proportion of food'.* This is not altogether true. The area that became the Soviet Zone was a relatively highly industrialized region. It contained not only part of Berlin, but also the industrial cities of Saxony and Thuringia. On the other hand, heathlands, much of their area now afforested, greatly reduced the area of

* Winston S. Churchill, *The Second World War*, vol. VI, p. 448.

crop-land, so that the Soviet-occupied Zone was in fact in a not much better situation than the Federal Republic in terms of food production. It was the area that has passed under Polish and Soviet administration that was in fact a food-surplus region. Parts of it were far from being good farm-land, and the agricultural practice was less advanced than has often been assumed. But it was, with a few significant exceptions, not an urbanized or industrialized area, and it was able to supply a limited range of foodstuffs to Central and West Germany. But the fact remains that no amount of ingenuity on the part of the German farmer could ever have made even these eastern lands supply the crops which West Germany most needs today. We shall return towards the end of this chapter to the question of the agricultural deficiencies of West Germany.

Agricultural Regions

In the meanwhile let us look at the agricultural possibilities of West Germany. Before the Middle Ages agriculture was not widely practised in Germany; the growing population then began to exert a pressure on the available crop-land, and during the following centuries the forest was gradually cleared from the better soils. Much of the loess area had probably been cultivated in prehistoric times; now the less tempting soils were brought under cultivation, until there remained only the poorest, the mountain soils, the heavy clays, and the light infertile sands and gravels. The long-drawn-out epic of forest clearance and settlement has left a deep impression on German folk-lore and legend. It was a great formative period in German history. The present pattern of villages was, in its essential features, the product of this period. The layout of farms and fields, so obstructive to modern agricultural developments, derives ultimately from this period, though modified during the following centuries.

The dominant influence on the present pattern of land use is the quality of the soil. Only a relatively small area of Germany has more than 50 per cent of its surface under cultivated crops.

This area is found, as might be expected, predominantly along the Upper Rhine from the Swiss border to Mainz, and along the borderland of the Central Uplands and northern plains, areas where the light and fertile loess was deposited by the winds of the glacial period. Other areas where arable land predominates are parts of the Neckar and Main valleys, where the varied rocks that lie in front of the Swabian and Franconian Jura have given rise to good soils, and parts of the Danube valley in Bavaria, where again there are areas of superior soils. By contrast, large areas are predominantly forested. These include the Bavarian Alps, the Black Forest, and Bavarian Forest, the Odenwald, Spessart, Thuringian Forest, and many parts of the Central Uplands. The sandy regions of the northern plain and the smaller areas of sand and gravel which occur in Bavaria, support heathland, which has occasionally been planted with coniferous forest, or improved sufficiently to provide rough grazing or to yield a crop of rye or potatoes. Intermediate in agricultural quality is much of South Germany, the less sandy areas of the northern plain, and many of the basins and depressions that mark the surface of the Central Uplands.

On the basis of these characteristics and contrasts it is possible to construct a series of agricultural regions. Seven of these are distinguished in Figure 9, and five of these are continued eastward through the Soviet Zone of Germany into the territory now under Polish administration. The nothern plain is divided into three regions on the basis of the soil and climate.

1. *North-western grass and fodder region.* This is a region of predominantly heavy soils, though it is also characterized by some restricted areas of sandy heath. It is also a region of relatively mild winters and cool summers and of great humidity. It is thus better suited to grass and fodder crops than to the cultivated cereals. A relatively large area is under pasture, and this region is perhaps most important as a dairying and pig-rearing area. The grain crops, of which rye is by far the most important, are partly used as animal feed.

2. *North-eastern rye and potato region.* This is distinguished from the first region by its rather greater extent of sandy heathland, and its drier and more continental climate. Winters are more severe. Dairy cattle can be left outdoors for shorter periods, and the growth of pasture is more interrupted. In consequence, permanent grassland is less extensive and important and cropland more important, though its quality is frequently poor. Meadow-land is maintained along the damp *Urstromtäler*, and forest is extensive over much of the intervening sandy areas. This type of country covers a great part of the Soviet Zone of Germany, and helps to explain its relatively low agricultural productivity.

3. *Baltic arable and dairy region.* Along the coast of the Baltic Sea, from the base of the Danish peninsula into the former East Prussia, is a region of boulder clay. It is a relatively narrow strip of land, stretching from the coast inland until it terminates against the belt of end moraines that marked a temporary halt in the retreat of the ice. Boulder clay soils are usually damp, heavy, and relatively difficult to plough. But they are potentially fertile owing to the variety of minerals that they represent, and sometimes require only to be drained in order to make good farmland. Cereal crops, especially rye and wheat, and potatoes and fodder crops are grown, and the latter are fed to cattle and pigs.

4. *Loess region.* This is by all odds the most valuable agricultural region in Germany. It lies as a discontinuous strip of land from Belgium in the west to central and eastern Germany. It widens in the great 'bay' of Cologne (Kölner Bucht) where the plain pushes southwards up the Rhine valley between the Eifel and the Bergische Land; then to the east it thins out, and is interrupted by ridges of highland thrust northwards into the plain. North of the Harz mountains it begins again and widens eastwards into Saxony and Silesia, curving round to the east and south of the Harz, and finally ending in the plain of Silesia. This is a rolling area. The land is almost entirely under cultivation; woodland has been cleared from all except the highest and

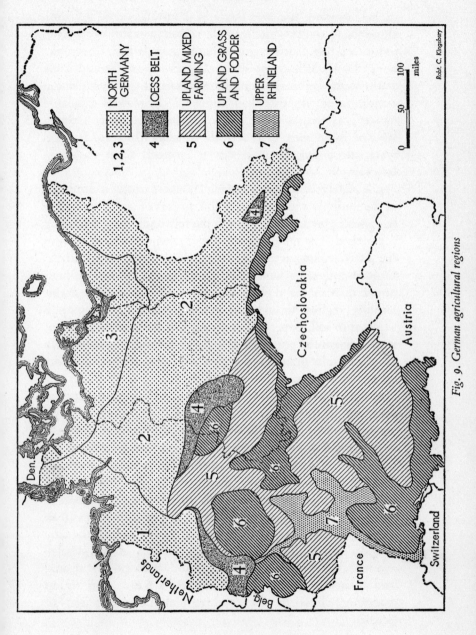

Fig. 9. German agricultural regions

Robt. C. Kingsbury

NORTH
GERMANY

LOESS BELT

UPLAND MIXED
FARMING

UPLAND GRASS
AND FODDER

UPPER
RHINELAND

1, 2, 3

4

5

6

7

steepest ground, and meadow and pasture are common only along the wetter floors of the valleys that cross the region from south to north. It is a region of large, prosperous villages, the houses huddled close together as if to take up as little as possible of the valuable soil. The crops are cereals, with wheat playing a more important role than in any of the regions examined hitherto, as well as sugar beet and potatoes. Cattle and pigs are not often seen in the fields. Usually they are stall-fed on potatoes and the pulp that is returned from the sugar factories.

5. *Upland mixed farming region.* The loess region is bordered in the south by a more hilly region, in part of which forest and hill grazing predominate, and in the remainder mixed farming is practised. The mixed farming area extends southward from the loess region, across the Central Uplands, and into the Danube valley. Its winters are more severe and its summers hotter than in the regions so far considered. It is an arable farming region, though the actual pattern of cropping is adjusted to soil, slope, and drainage. On the better soils wheat is grown; on the poorer, oats and rye are most common. On all of them the grain crops are grown in rotation with fodder crops and potatoes.

6. *Upland grass and forest region.* This is a fragmented region, made up of those areas of the upland belt which are high enough to have a particularly cool or severe climate, or have so poor a soil that crop-farming is uneconomic. It embraces the mainly wooded uplands of the appropriately named Sauerland; the high moors of the Eifel, the forested Harz mountains, the Black Forest, and the wooded hills that lie along the border of Bohemia. These regions are heavily forested; in some areas, such as the Black Forest, considerably more than half the land is under forest. Although there are patches of crop-land— commonly rye, potatoes, and hardy fodder crops—the cleared land is mostly devoted to pasture. As a whole, this region contributes little to the total agricultural production of Germany.

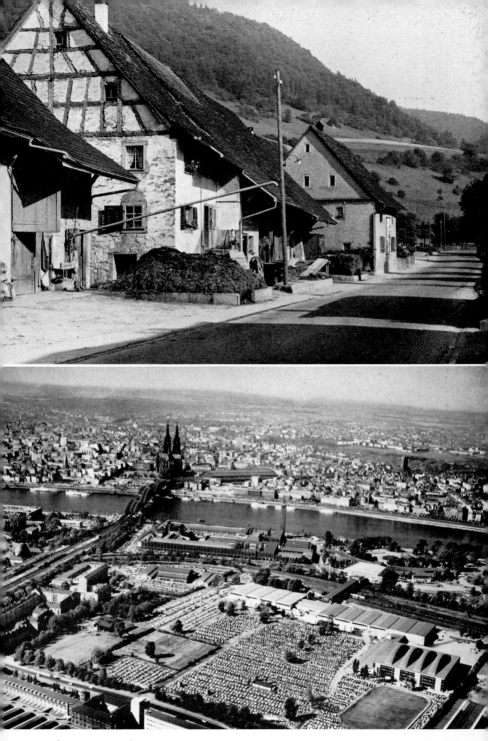

9. *A farm in Württemberg*

10. *Cologne* (Köln), *seen looking west across the Rhine. To the right of the Cathedral is the central railway station*

11. *The new face of Düsseldorf*

12. Wuppertal lies along the twisting valley of the Wupper, and the overhead railway—the Schwebebahn, is suspended over the river, parallel with the city's main street

13. The main shopping street of West Berlin, and symbol of its prosperity, is the Kurfürstendamm. In the distance is the Gedächtniskirche, built as a memorial to the first Kaiser, and preserved in its ruined condition as a reminder of the Second World War and the bombing

14. *One of the most attractively rebuilt areas of Berlin is the Hansa Quarter (Hansaviertel) here seen from the top of the Siegessäule, on the western edge of the Tiergarten*

Included in this upland grazing and forest region is the small section of the Alps that lies within southern Germany. Here the climatic characteristics of the upland region are intensified: summers are cool; winters cold, and rainfall heavy. Crop-farming scarcely extends beyond the growing of a few fodder crops for the winter feed of the animals. A limited form of transhumance is still practised here. In order to free the valley pastures in summer for a crop of hay, many of the cattle are sent up the mountains to the Alpine pastures, from which they descend in the autumn, to spend the winters in their owners' stables, where hay and fodder have been accumulated for them. Naturally, the chief agricultural product of this region is dairy produce, much of it in the form of butter and cheese, which can be stored and transported most easily.

7. *Upper Rhineland.* The small Upper Rhineland region, reaching from near Mainz upstream to the Swiss border, is another area of relatively high fertility, and it also received a dusting of loess. It has more sunshine, and enjoys a shorter winter and hotter summer than the more northerly region. Much of this region is suited for the cultivation of wheat and sugar beet; it is also suited to the more valuable vineyards and fruit orchards that cover much of its surface.

The Structure of Agriculture

The structure of agriculture in western and southern Germany is today dominated by the small farm. In the main it is a land of peasant farmers. What is now the Soviet Zone, on the other hand, had formerly been characterized in part by large estates, but these, after having been in some degree broken up and distributed among the peasants, have now been forcibly collectivized (see p. 59). In 1960–1, 3·3 million persons were permanently employed on the land in the Federal Republic; of these about 0·3 million were farmworkers; the rest were farm owners and members of their families. This in itself suggests that the average size of the farms was small. A recent survey

(1961) showed that out of almost 1·6 million farms, about 28 per cent were of less than 5 acres:

Under 2 hectares	450,700 farms
2–5 hectares	371,600
5–10 hectares	336,600
10–20 hectares	289,500
20–50 hectares	123,800
Over 50 hectares	16,500
	1,588,700

Almost two-thirds of the farms, covering 37 per cent of the cultivated land, were by English standards uneconomically small.

The inconvenience of small farms is intensified by the fragmented nature of most of them. 'Of all the afflictions of the European farmer,' wrote P. Lamartine Yates,* 'fragmentation must be reckoned the worst.' A small farm holding of, say, 10 acres might be divided into several times as many plots. The farmer follows his own desires in cultivating each, thus giving to the landscape a rich and varied quality of many-hued greens in spring and of yellows and browns in summer. But the disadvantages of this system are as conspicuous as its scenic pattern. The fragments of land 'are of various shapes, some long and narrow, some not even rectilinear. Only a few abut on a road or cart track; most have to be reached by walking along the edge of other people's plots. This often precludes the use of even simple machines such as binders, not to mention tractors. It impedes weed control and crop spraying; and since the land is unfenced it prevents the running of animals on the stubbles except they be herded.' This system, with its infinitely complex patterns, is a product of the tenurial system, whereby a farmer's holding is divided equally between his children on his death. Only too often the most equitable division—the division of

* P. Lamartine Yates, *Food, Land, and Manpower in Western Europe*, London, 1960, p. 174.

each parcel of land into the necessary number of fragments—is also the least economic. It has been estimated that some 16 million acres—nearly a half of the total—stood in urgent need of consolidation into larger and more compact parcels of land.* In South Germany the problem is very much more acute than in North, and in Bavaria, it has been said, 75 per cent of the land requires consolidation. The Agricultural Ministry of the Federal Government has adopted a long-term policy of consolidating the excessively fragmented farms and of increasing the size of the smaller and less economic. Over a period of fifteen years it plans to consolidate 15 million acres of farmland. This task is, however, beset with difficulties. It is hard to achieve a new division of the crop-land of the village that satisfies its members, and equally difficult to convince so conservative a body of the desirability of such a change.

Before the political unification of Germany agricultural products had enjoyed some degree of protection. Tariffs on imported foodstuffs, predominantly cereals, were abolished for a time, but were restored at a higher level in 1879. This was done in view of the cheapness, on the one hand, of imported cereals, aided by the expanding means of bulk transport, and, on the other, of the high indebtedness of the German farmer. The effect of the tariff was clearly to increase the price of food to the industrial worker; it may also have served in some degree to insulate a traditional pattern of agriculture from the foreign competition which had brought about fundamental changes in the agriculture of the United Kingdom, Denmark, and the Netherlands, and to slow down its modernization. In recent years, however, there has been a rapid improvement in its technical level. The number of tractors, for example, increased sixfold between 1950 and 1960, from 139,000 to 857,000. Even so, it was estimated in 1955 that 80 per cent of the farms still did not have the use of a tractor. Other types of farm machinery —milking machines, combines, threshing machines, beet

* 'The Federal Republic of Germany', *Overseas Economic Surveys.* H.M.S.O., 1955.

harvesters—have recently increased rapidly in number. But much progress has still to be made if the German farmer is to be equipped as well as some of his competitors in other member states of the European Common Market. The government programme for agriculture, the so-called Green Plan, already mentioned, provides also for long-term loans to the farmer for equipment and improvements and for building more housing for farmworkers in those areas where it is desirable to attract farm labour. It also encourages the concentration of scattered holdings and the erection of new farm buildings, centrally located on a compact farm.

The German farmer has always made a heavy use of fertilizers, partly because Germany has been for over a century a leading producer of the heavy chemicals, and partly because the government, through its control of prices, has made it possible for the farmer to use them. The consumption of the more important fertilizers is now appreciably higher per hectare than before the war, and this is an important factor in the relatively high crop yields now obtained in Germany.

Farm incomes are relatively low in Germany, and in recent years the price of farm products has risen less sharply than that of the industrial and consumers' goods which the farmer has to buy. The farmers' indebtedness has tended to increase. In the words of a recent report on economic and commercial conditions in the Federal Republic, 'Eighty years of isolation and protectionism have seen German husbandry decline from the high standards of a few generations ago to relative backwardness. Guaranteed markets and prices, high Customs tariffs and import quotas, have produced a situation today in which only the employment of public funds on a large scale and over a period of years can make good the neglect of decades.'* This is the object of the Ministry's plan for German agriculture.

Yet, despite these adverse conditions, agriculture in Germany has made great progress in recent years. The yields of the

* 'The Federal Republic of Germany', *Overseas Economic Surveys*, H.M.S.O., 1955, p. 154.

important crops have increased not only above the relatively low level of ten years ago, but also above that of the pre-war years. Production of the more important grain crops has been:

	1935–8* average	1952	1954	1956	1957	1958	1960
Wheat	2,515	3,291	2,892	3,490	3,870	3,721	4,965
Rye	3,017	3,119	4,098	3,748	3,838	3,748	3,791
Barley	1,723	1,757	1,920	2,326	2,513	2,423	3,221
Oats	2,826	2,616	2,473	2,485	2,250	2,172	2,178

(in thousands of metric tons)

Certain trends are apparent from these figures. One is the sharp increase in the bread grains, wheat and rye, and the more than proportionate increase in wheat. This has been accompanied by only a minute increase in the area under these crops, and is accounted for mainly by heavier yields. The increase in yields per hectare have been quite remarkable:

	1935–8 average	1952	1954	1958	1960
Wheat	2·23	2·76	2·61	2·68	3·29
Rye	1·83	2·3	2·68	2·49	2·88
Barley	2·12	2·49	2·62	2·75	3·29
Oats	2·07	2·35	2·62	2·59	2·91

(in metric tons per hectare)

The greater increase in wheat production reflects a change in consumer demand. The West German is eating more wheat bread than he did even a few years ago, and wheat imports have also increased sharply to meet this need. The increase which is also shown in rye production is accounted for by the fact that considerable areas are not suitable for producing any superior grain, and that increasing quantities of rye are fed to the stock. Oats, grown exclusively as a fodder crop, has shown a steady diminution in crop area, and now is sown on less than two-thirds of the area which it occupied before the Second World War. This is a reflection in part of the slowly

* Production for the area now comprising the Federal Republic of Germany.

diminishing number of horses, for which it provided the chief fodder; in part of the decline of crop-farming in those hilly regions where it was formerly an important crop.

Potatoes occupy the biggest area after the grain crops. They have many uses. They form an important item in human diet, though one that, in the present prosperous conditions, is tending to diminish in importance as diet comes to take in more protein and to exclude some of its formerly heavy starch content. They provide an industrial raw material for distilling and starch-making, and the remainder are fed to pigs. The area under potatoes has declined slightly, though the total crop remains somewhat above the pre-war average:

	1938	1956	1958	1961
Area under potatoes (1,000's of hectares)	1,192	1,148	1,073	976
Yield of potatoes (1,000's of metric tons)	21,594	26,999	22,855	21,504

Seed potatoes, for sowing in most parts of Germany, were formerly grown in large quantities on the sandy soils of the east, and the division of Germany caused, temporarily at least, a serious shortage of potatoes for planting.

Livestock farming has shown a sharp increase in size and importance. During the war years stock had been depleted, and a shortage of feed reduced the yield of milk and meat. Since then the numbers of cattle and pigs have been restored to their pre-war level and in some instances have exceeded them.

The number of pigs and poultry greatly exceeds the pre-war level, and that of cattle is slightly higher. This again reflects the change that has taken place in recent years in the food habits of the German people. Consumption of meat, milk, and animal fats has increased at the expense of bread and potatoes. The total dairy herd is now somewhat larger than before the war, and the average milk yield of each cow considerably higher. This reflects the adequacy of the local production of animal feed and the improving quality of the dairy herds themselves. There remains, perhaps inevitably, a regional contrast in the milk yields. Dairy cattle in North Germany, where the climate is damper and the growing season for grass longer, yield on average about 50 per cent more milk than those in the drier, more continental south of Germany. In addition to the northern plain, the hills of the Alpine Foreland, notably the Allgäu region, are very important for the production of milk. The consumption of liquid milk is increasing, and it might be assumed that farmers, especially in those areas best suited to dairy farming, will grow more fodder crops and less bread crops. Production and consumption of butter and cheese have increased less sharply than those of liquid milk, and domestic production is generally sufficient to cover most of the local demand.

Production and consumption of eggs has also increased sharply during the past decade, though domestic production remains insufficient, especially in winter, to cover the demand. There has been a large seasonal import of eggs in spite of a tariff protection for the German poultry industry. The fact that this competition has come mainly from Denmark and the Netherlands is of particular importance to the German farmer who sees his economic position threatened even more by Germany's membership in the European Common Market.

The consumption of fruit and vegetables has also increased since the war, and is now very considerably above the pre-war level. To a large extent this increase has been in imported and tropical fruits which could not possibly be produced in Germany; but there has at the same time been an improvement in the domestic production of fruit and vegetables. This has in part resulted from better care of fruit orchards and a more intensive cultivation of market gardens. The chief fruit-growing areas are in south and south-west Germany, where the summers are hotter and more sunny than in the rest of this country. Vegetables are grown in the vicinity of every city, large and small, and assume a very great importance in the region of Cologne and in the Upper Rhineland. Production has hitherto been protected by a tariff on imported vegetables, but demand has fluctuated, and it is said that such traditional German foods as red and white cabbage have declined in importance.

Sugar beet is by far the most important industrial crop in West Germany. Its cultivation had been stepped up during the pre-war years when Germany was striving for self-sufficiency in foodstuffs. Since the war the acreage under sugar beet has, until very recently, continued to increase and the yield per hectare has been improved:

	1938	1956	1958	1960
Sugar beet:				
Area (1,000's of hectares)	159	269	284	260
Yield (1,000's of metric tons)	5,232	8,348	11,237	9,693

The sugar beet is a useful crop. It adjusts easily to a crop rotation; its tops make a useful fodder, and the pulp that comes back from the beet factory provides additional animal feed. Its cultivation thus fits well into the prevailing trend in German agriculture to produce more meat and milk and less bread crops.

This trend is illustrated by the changes that have taken place since the war in the source of farm income:

	1935–9	1949–50 million		1956–7 million		1960–1 million	
	%	DM	%	DM	%	DM	%
Farm income arising from:							
Crop husbandry	31·6	3,575	31·1	5,303	26·8	6,500	27·8
Animal husbandry	68·4	7,928	68·9	13,773	73·2	16,850	72·2
	100	11,503	100	19,076	100	23,350	100

This table shows a slight trend away from grain crops and towards fodder crops and animal husbandry.

Viticulture is dominated by tradition and is less responsive to market conditions than almost every other branch of agriculture. The long-established vineyards along the middle and upper valley of the Rhine and the Mosel valley have been better tended in recent years. The yield and quality depend so much on the weather of the previous summer that it is almost impossible to isolate the influence of policy and market on the one hand from that of natural circumstances on the other. There has, however, been a contraction in the total area under vines. This seems to have been a result of the abandonment of many very small vineyards, some of them run as a part-time occupation, in parts of the Rhineland, Franconia, and Swabia.

Co-operative societies have been important in German agriculture ever since they were first established in the nineteenth century by Raiffeisen. They were temporarily suppressed by the Nazis, but revived after the war, and their membership today includes most of the independent farmers. About three-quarters of the dairy produce is now marketed by the co-operatives, together with a considerable proportion of the grain and vegetables. The societies provide also for the collective purchase of fertilizer and the joint use of farm machinery. The co-operative organization does a great deal to counteract the disadvantages of very small farm holdings.

Agriculture in the Economy of the Federal Republic of Germany

It will have been inferred from the previous pages that agriculture is one of the least efficient sectors of the German economy. This is borne out by the size of its contribution to the total income. Before 1950 agriculture provided employment for over 20 per cent of the active population, but contributed some 12 per cent of the net national product. Productivity in agriculture has increased considerably in recent years, but its growth has been far slower than that of other sectors of the economy. It now contributes less than 10 per cent of the net national product, while employing still about 14 per cent of the labour force.

It remains to examine the degree of self-sufficiency in German agriculture and the extent to which this situation has been affected by the loss of the Eastern Territories and the division of Germany into East and West. The percentages of total requirements produced within Germany during the years immediately preceding the Second World War, in 1955–6 and in 1960–1, are given below. These figures show the immense progress towards self-sufficiency that has been made in the Federal Republic:

	1935–6 to 1938–9	1955–6	1960–1
	%	%	%
Wheat	65	54	75
Rye	89	99	99
Sugar	51	80	90
Potatoes	96	99	98
Meat	93	91	84
Milk	100	100	100
Cheese	87	70	61
All fats	58	44	49
Fresh fruit	98	68	83
Vegetables	91	81	74

West Germany is today somewhat less dependent upon imported cereals than Germany as a whole was before the First or even the Second World War. The Federal Republic has a small deficit in sugar instead of the surplus which characterized pre-war Germany. This clearly reflects the loss of the eastern lands and the severance of the Federal Republic from the sugar-beet producing regions of the former province of Saxony (Sachsen). The changes indicated in these tables must be viewed against the increased density of population in West Germany on the one hand and the changes in diet on the other. Wheat is now relatively more important than it formerly was, though the starch foods as a whole now play a smaller role, and meat, milk and milk products, in which there is a near self-sufficiency, are assuming a greater importance.

In contrast with the agriculture of West Germany, that in the Soviet-occupied Zone and in the Polish and Soviet-held territory has passed through revolutionary changes which have altered fundamentally both the appearance of the landscape and the structure of farming. These areas of Germany had been in part characterized by great estates. Immediately after the war most of these—in the Soviet-occupied Zone, all over 100 hectares—were broken up and the land distributed amongst the poor or landless peasants. In the territory east of the Oder and Neisse a few estates were retained as state-operated farms, and the rest distributed among the Polish immigrants who had come to replace the former German population.

Collectivization never made much progress in the Polish-occupied area, but in that part of East Prussia annexed by the Soviet Union collectivization appears to have been imposed at once. In the Soviet-occupied area of Germany a few co-operatives were formed, but a thorough programme of collectivization was not introduced until 1952. By 1960, it was claimed that all land was socially owned, except the half-hectare holdings that the peasant families were allowed to retain for their own use.

Collectivization has brought with it extensive changes. There has been a flight from the land of peasants anxious to escape this form of regimentation; mechanization of agriculture has been intensified so that 'Middle' Germany now has a more highly mechanized agriculture than West; the familiar pattern of small cultivated strips has been replaced by one of large, compact fields. The pattern of cropping has also changed: the area under grain has diminished, and that under fodder crops has increased. The yield per acre has in some instances fallen below the level of the 1930s, and in no instance has it improved greatly on that level. In general it is below, sometimes—as in the case of sugar beet—very far below the level of the Federal Republic.

Animal husbandry has increased in importance, and the numbers of all categories of farm-stock, except horses, have increased. This, of course, reflects the increasing area under fodder crops.

The Soviet-occupied Zone is today no area of food surplus, and, despite its diminished population, actually imports considerable quantities of bread grains and also of other foodstuffs.

4

Industrial Development

In the late eighteenth century industry in the United Kingdom was moving from workshop to factory; steam power was replacing water power, and the iron industry, which had hitherto prospered in the forested regions, was being re-established on the coalfields. At this time Germany was made up of between three and four hundred states, ranging in size from large and viable units, like Prussia and Bavaria, to small states of only a few square miles. Though nominally part of the Holy Roman Empire, they were for practical purposes sovereign and independent. They surrounded themselves with tariff walls. Trade was stultified by the multiplicity of customs barriers and hindered by tolls levied on rivers and roads. No revolution in industry, comparable to that which was taking place in England, was possible, and some of the technical inventions which had been made in England took up to a century to reach Germany.

After the fall of Napoleon, in 1815, the map of Germany was re-fashioned. The number of states was reduced to only thirty-nine, and thus their size increased. Soon after this, the initial steps were taken in the creation of a *Zollverein*, or Customs Union. Progress was slow, but the completion of the process, some fifty years later, created in Germany a single market for the products of industry and agriculture.

The creation of the Zollverein was accompanied by the building of a railway net. This resulted in part from private initiative, in part from that of the states, many of which built and operated their own lines. Fortunately a uniform gauge was adopted, so that these lines could ultimately be absorbed into a single railway system. The important fact is that in Germany, unlike England, the construction of a railway net preceded the development of a modern factory industry. In the English industrial experience, the problem of transporting industrial fuels and raw materials had been in the early days a very serious one, and industries had been attracted to the coalfields which supplied their fuel. In Germany, too, coalfields exercised a strong attraction, especially for the iron and steel industries, but the prior existence of railways encouraged a wider dispersion of industry than could possibly have occurred in Great Britain during the early phases of its industrial growth.

At the time when the Zollverein was completed and the German Empire had come to replace the loose and ineffective Confederation (1871), the bulk of German industrial production was carried out on a craft basis, reminiscent more of Hans Sachs's workshop than of the smoking factories of contemporary England. Yet, within a generation, Germany had transformed itself from a predominantly rural and agricultural to a mainly urban and industrial country. Between the formation of the German Empire and the outbreak of the First World War, the urban population of Germany had increased from one-third to two-thirds of a total which had itself increased by over 50 per cent in the period. At the end of this period factory manufacture was normal in most branches of industry, and the hand-spinners, the handloom weavers, and craftsmen of all kinds were rapidly disappearing from the German scene. Indeed Germany tended to go to the opposite extreme, and, by the formation of cartels, to build up concentrations of industry, with a unified system of control, that would have been inconceivable before the formation of the German Empire.

The geography of German industry forms three consecutive patterns, each adjusted to the contemporary technology. In the first, industries were carried on, mainly on a craft basis, only in the older cities. Their raw materials derived mainly from the local region, and their chief market was in the surrounding countryside. The industrial regions of earlier Germany were, by and large, the richer agricultural regions, because there alone was to be found a population large and rich enough to support them. The only exception lay in the mining and metallurgical industries which sought the hills that supplied both ore and charcoal and furnished also power from their running streams.

A change came with the introduction of steam power. Despite the early development of a network of communication, heavy industry was attracted to the sources of mineral fuel, and Germany, like Great Britain, developed highly industrialized regions on or very close to the coalfields. The foremost of such regions were the Ruhr, the Saar, and Upper Silesia. Most of the iron, steel, and mechanical engineering industries came to be located in these regions, together with much of the chemical and part of the textile industries.

The last phase in the geographical evolution of the pattern of industry is characterized by a new dispersion. To some extent this had been made possible by the transport of solid fuel by river and canal as well as by rail. But with the growing use of electric power and of gas in industry an even wider distribution of manufacturing became possible. Today a light industry can be established in almost any part of Germany without encountering difficulties in the supply of power, either from hydro-electric generators built along the rivers or from thermal stations located on the brown or bituminous coalfields. The network of gas pipelines, conveying in a few instances natural gas, but mainly coal-gas from coke ovens built on the coalfields, is less extensive, but is nevertheless also a factor in the dispersion of industry. Even less developed at present are the petroleum pipelines. In addition to the refineries already built along the Rhine it is planned also to establish refineries in Bavaria and to supply them by means of pipelines from the Mediterranean coast. These will in turn supply both oil fuel and petroleum by-products to industries located far from the coalfield in South Germany.

The rapid industrial growth in Germany has been without precedent at any time or in any place. It found in the late nineteenth-century Germany peculiarly favourable conditions.

In the first place, the State, both the German Empire and its constituent states, continued through the nineteenth century to pursue the paternalistic policy that had characterized many of them in the eighteenth, whereas, in Great Britain, the Government had, in effect, renounced any close control over industry and related fields, such as transport, considering that the best interests of the State were served by the self-interest of the entrepreneur; Germany at no time succumbed to so thorough-going a doctrine of *laissez-faire*. The nearest approach to it was made in the 1870s, but this experiment was short-lived, and with the introduction of its new scale of tariffs in 1879, the German Empire demonstrated that it would itself ensure the proper conditions for the growth of the industries which it favoured.

The high level of tariff protection, which from this date characterized most branches of German industry, succeeded in excluding foreign competition from the German market. This sheltered atmosphere encouraged, if it did not promote, the growth of cartels. Their object was to maintain remunerative price-levels for German industrial products, and their purpose was furthered by the relative absence of outside competition. An extraordinary feature of German development during this period is that protection did not lead to stagnation. We have already seen that German agriculture, which was also highly protected, became one of the least progressive sectors of the economy. It is not easy to explain why industry reacted differently. Partial explanations are to be found in the level of scientific and technical education, which was probably higher than that in Great Britain throughout much of the century. A second contributory factor was the prestige and social status which soon came to attach to industrial management, and a third was the readiness of the German to experiment and to innovate. In spite of its closeness in time to the hidebound craft industries of the pre-industrial age, no body of industrial entrepreneurs, not even the Japanese, showed a greater readiness to change their organization and their processes, and, at the same time, a greater receptivity to developments made in other countries.

A simple example drawn from the history of the German iron and steel industry may serve to illustrate the change that came over German industry in the second half of the nineteenth century. In 1709 the process of using metallurgical coke in the smelting of iron was first used successfully in England. Later in the century it was tried in France, and at the end was introduced into Upper Silesia by English technicians under the auspices of the Prussian Government. It was not adopted in the Ruhr, the area best suited to employ it, until 1849, just 140 years after its invention in England. This slowness to adopt a process whose advantages were obvious is not easy to explain. But in marked contrast with this is the German reaction to the English invention of the basic or Gilchrist-Thomas process of steel-making. The success of Thomas's experiments at a steelworks in South Wales was made public in 1879. Within a week or two German steel companies, the Hoerder Verein and the Rheinische Stahlwerke, had dispatched emissaries to Thomas to secure German rights in his patent, and the one who travelled through the night without resting was the one who got to him first. Within a further period of only five months a basic steel charge was first blown in Germany. This enterprising, inquiring spirit, as ready to introduce new methods as to search out new markets, stands in sharp contrast to the lack of progress and change in German agriculture.

Attitudes among the German entrepreneurs and people encouraged these developments, but, even so, Germany might not have progressed either as far or as fast if Nature had not been in some ways particularly generous. The agricultural endowment of Germany, it is true, was not over-great, and the German people did not in fact make the best use of what they had. But their mineral endowment was handsome and in many respects gave them an advantage over their neighbours and competitors. Furthermore, the natural conditions favoured water-borne traffic and added the advantages of easy river and canal transport to those furnished by the early development of a railway net.

In many ways the coalfields of Germany were the basis of German industrial growth, and industrial expansion was accompanied by a rapid expansion of coal production. From a total output of less than 30 million tons of bituminous coal in 1871, production rose to over 190 million tons on the eve of the First World War, forty-four years later. This was paralleled by an even more rapid increase in the production of lignite. Most important by far were the Ruhr and Upper Silesian coalfields, which together contained about 97 per cent of total reserves and accounted for almost as large a percentage of the total output before the First World War. The structure and resources of the Ruhr coalfield have already been described. Germany in 1921 had to cede part of the Upper Silesian coalfield to Poland, and the sector of the coal basin which remained German was in 1945 also occupied by Poland. Of the remaining coalfields that of the Saar was the largest and most important. A series of small coal basins lay along the border of the Central Uplands and the northern plain or just within the hills, from the Dutch and Belgian border in the west to Silesia in the east. Mining was developed and became locally important near Aachen, near Hanover in Lower Saxony, near Chemnitz and Zwickau in Upper Saxony, and in Lower Silesia. Of these coal basins that of Lower Silesia—often called the Waldenburg coalfield— is within territory now administered by Poland and the Upper Saxon field is now in the Soviet Zone.

The Federal Republic of Germany today contains the Ruhr, Aachen, Lower Saxon, and Saar coalfields, which together contribute a major share of the total production from all German coalfields.

COAL PRODUCTION (1960)
in metric tons

Federal Republic of Germany	143,255,000
Soviet Zone	2,721,000
Territory now under Polish administration	30,000,000 (est.)

The West German production in 1961 was made up of:

		%
The Ruhr	116,083,000	81·3
Aachen	8,356,000	5·9
Lower Saxony	2,211,000	1·5
Saarland	16,090,000	11·3
	142,740,000	100·0

These fields, producing a wide range of types of coal, do not exhaust the fuel resources of Germany. Germany probably has the largest reserves of any country in the world of brown coal or lignite. This is found in thick deposits which extend over large areas and occur at depths which are generally so shallow that open-cast mining is practicable. The largest lignite fields are in Saxony, between the cities of Merseburg and Halle, and

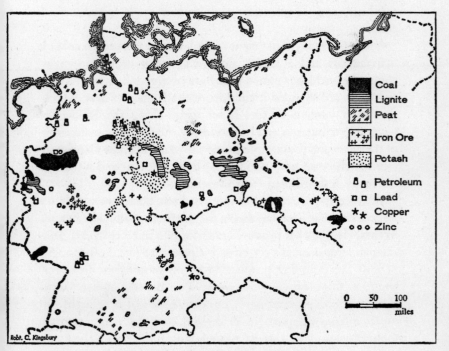

Fig. 10. The industrial resources of Germany

67

in Nieder Lausitz, all in the Soviet Zone. Other fields, hitherto but little developed, lie east of the Oder river, in the area now under Polish administration. The only large brown coalfields in West Germany lie to the west and south-west of Cologne. Their importance has been overshadowed by that of the Ruhr coalfield, and the quality of the coal is somewhat lower than that of the brown coal deposits in the Soviet Zone. The better qualities of brown coal from the Lower Rhineland are used mainly for briquetting, while the poorer are burned in electric generators built close to the huge open pits. In the Soviet Zone use of the brown coal reserves has been more fully developed, chiefly because the amount of bituminous coal obtained locally is quite small. Here the lignite is used not only to generate power, but also as a basis of chemical industries and of synthetic oil production, as in the Schwarze Pumpe combine, and as the source of a low-grade metallurgical coke.

South Germany is deficient in coal, except the brown coal of Schwandorf and a low-quality bituminous coal, known as Pechkohle, which is mined near Persenburg, and its homes and industries are supplied mainly from the Ruhr and Saar. Much of the movement of fuel is by barge along the Rhine, its navigable tributaries and its subsidiary canals. The canalization of the Main and the completion of the Main-Danube Canal will increase the ease with which coal from western and northern Germany is distributed to the south.

Petroleum occurs, as has already been noted, in a belt of territory which stretches across the northern plain. The extent of these deposits has become better known in recent years, and their development is very largely a post-war phenomenon. At present the domestic production of oil is sufficient to cover about a third of German needs. For the remainder West Germany is dependent upon imports, much of it brought by pipeline from the ports of Wilhelmshaven and Rotterdam to the refineries located near Cologne, but in the future these are expected to be supplemented by petroleum piped from the

Mediterranean ports of Marseilles and Genoa to refineries in South Germany.

Of all the metalliferous minerals, iron ore is by far the most important to modern industry. West Germany has large reserves but most of these are of low grade, and have been exploited only in recent years. There were a number of small deposits of high-grade ore, especially in the hills of the Siegerland, in the Lahn-Dill region, in the Oberpfalzer Jura, and elsewhere. Though sometimes of very high quality, these ore bodies were generally very restricted in size. They were the basis of small but locally important iron-smelting industries in the eighteenth and nineteenth centuries, but the ores are now largely exhausted, and the industries that were based on them are in most instances closed. The modern German iron industry is based mainly on good quality imported ores. A large part of these has been furnished by Sweden. They are brought by freighter from the Norwegian or Swedish ports to the coast of north-west Europe, and from there are carried, mainly by barge, to the ironworks. In 1871 Germany annexed Alsace and a large part of Lorraine, and held these territories until the end of the First World War. Lorraine contains the largest reserves of iron ore in Europe, and, at the time when it was annexed by Germany, they had already begun to be exploited by the French. A few years after Germany had occupied Lorraine, the discovery of the basic process of making steel, which made it easier to use an iron with a high phosphorus content in the steel furnace, gave an entirely new value to the Lorraine ores. They quickly became the most important source of iron ore within the boundaries of Germany as these existed at the time. But the Lorraine ore was never transported far. It was a low-grade ore, rarely containing more than about 30 per cent iron, and thus could not justify the expense of a long railway journey. In consequence it was mostly smelted in Lorraine itself. Much of the fuel needed for the process was supplied from the Ruhr, but Lorraine itself never sent much ore to the Ruhr. Instead, it distributed rolled steel goods and other half-finished products of the steel mills to many parts of Germany. After 1918 Lorraine ceased to be part of Germany, but the former industrial relationship between Germany and Lorraine gains interest and importance from the fact that a new commercial link between the two is in process of being forged (see Chapter 6).

Ores similar to those of Lorraine occur in very large quantities to the north and north-west of the Harz mountains. Like those of Lorraine, they are highly phosphoric, and have a low metal content. Although these ores had been smelted locally on a small scale during the late nineteenth century, as at Peine, they were not widely used until the National Socialist drive for self-sufficiency led to a renewed interest in them. In the 1930s a large plant was built at Salzgitter to prepare and smelt the ore. Though dismantled at the end of the war, it has since been rebuilt, and is now a source of pig-iron and rolled steel goods. Some ore from the Salzgitter area is also being sent to the Ruhr.

In the later Middle Ages and early modern times Germany was one of the most important mining countries in the then known world. It was an important source of lead and silver, and other metals were known to exist. But the reserves were small and many deposits have since been exhausted and the mines closed. Small quantities of lead, zinc, and copper continue, however, to be mined. Most of the present production comes from the Harz mountains, the Siegerland, and the Lahn-Dill region, the scene of one of the earliest metalliferous mines in Europe, but production from the Eifel has now ceased. A greater importance today attaches to the deposits of potash and common salt. These occur over a wide area lying to the north, east, and south of the Harz mountains. The more intensively developed reserves lie in Saxony, in the Soviet Zone, but important resources extend north-westward through the Harz Foreland into Lower Saxony.

Industrial Regions

On the basis of these resources, aided by an effective transport network, the Germans have developed during the past century a number of industrial regions. Each is an area within which factory industries provide the most important single source of employment, and each has a fairly wide range of industry. Two such industrial regions have grown up around the North Sea ports of Bremen and Hamburg. Two more, including the North Rhine-Westphalian industrial region, which embraces the Ruhr, have developed over the border between the Central Uplands and the northern plain. Six more regions can be distinguished in central and south Germany: the Saarland; the Rhine-Main region, including Frankfurt and Mainz; the Rhine-Neckar region, including Mannheim, Ludwigshafen and Worms; the Swabian industrial region, including Stuttgart and Heilbronn; and the Nuremberg and Munich-Augsburg regions. To these must, of course, be added the industrial region of Berlin. Mention must also be made of German industrial regions lying beyond the boundaries of the Federal Republic, particularly Upper Saxony and Thuringia, the Baltic ports, and Central and Upper Silesia. These regions are illustrated in Figure 11. In the following paragraphs the dominant industrial characteristics of each are examined.

The North Sea Ports. It is a tribute to their great prestige and to their importance in German economic life that the port cities of Bremen and Hamburg are constituted as two separate *Länder* in the Federal Republic. Hamburg has long been the chief maritime outlet for Central Europe, with much of which it is connected by the river Elbe and its tributary canals and rivers. It is less favourably placed to serve western Germany than central and eastern, nevertheless it remains the chief port of the Federal Republic. Hamburg has attracted the range of industries that commonly develop in a port. Shipbuilding is the foremost. Shipyards line the river Elbe below the city, and the electrical and engineering industries that are tributary to shipbuilding are well developed. But Hamburg has also developed those industries which are based especially on bulky imported raw materials, most conveniently processed near the dockside before being distributed. These include oil-refining, the processing of imported vegetable oils, and the manufacture of soap, margarine, and related goods; the milling of imported grain, the smelting of imported ores, and the preparation of imported tobacco.

The industries of Bremen and its vicinity are generally similar, though their scale is smaller. To these, however, it adds the processing of textile raw materials. Bremen has long been the chief port of entry for raw wool, cotton, jute, and other fibres. Some are spun and woven here; others are cleaned, combed, or otherwise prepared for the consuming factories inside Germany. It is also the chief centre for the import and roasting of coffee, which spreads its agreeable aroma over parts of the city.

North Rhine-Westphalia. This is the largest both in its area and in the volume of its industrial production in Germany, and is, by all standards of measurement, the most important in the national economy. Its heart is near the junction of the little river Ruhr with the Rhine, but it spreads west to the Belgian and Dutch borders; it extends up the Rhine to Cologne, and spreads out over the hills of the western Sauerland and the Bergische Land; it includes the textile centre of Wuppertal and the steel and engineering city of Hagen. To the north it reaches out into the plain to embrace the cities of Münster and Bocholt. It covers some 5,000 square miles and contains at least ten million people.

Today the life-blood of this region is drawn from the coal mines of the Ruhr, but this was an industrial and commercial region long before the coal mines of the Ruhr gained importance. The Rhine was, during the Middle Ages, one of the most frequented of Europe's highways of commerce, and Cologne was at that time one of the largest cities of the Continent. By medieval standards the area was already highly urbanized. Crafts were carried on in the cities, and in the hilly margins of the Sauerland and Eifel iron ore was dug, smelted, and refined by the slow, simple processes of the period. Indeed, it is highly probable that it was in this general region that the blast furnace

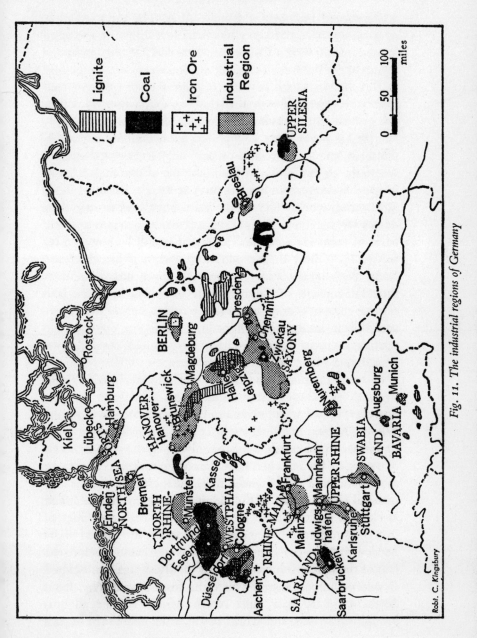

Fig. 11. The industrial regions of Germany

73

was invented in the later Middle Ages. The early smelting operations were carried on with charcoal as their fuel, and were located mainly within the forested Central Uplands. The opening up of the Ruhr coalfield, and the discovery here, in the first half of the nineteenth century, of a good quality coking coal merely brought about a gradual shift of the iron industry within this general area. It declined in the hills, as it grew on the coalfield. It has never quite disappeared from the hilly region. A few blast furnaces remain in operation near Siegen, but elsewhere the closing down of the multitude of diminutive blast-furnaces and refineries has left, as their legacy, a host of small metal-using works. They make nails, bolts, and screws; they draw wire, fashion locks and keys, and make small iron castings. Most of them are very small; a few may still be powered by water. They draw their crude metal and their fuel from the Ruhr. Their local advantages now amount to little more than their fixed plant, the human skills assembled here, and the relative cheapness of living amid the rolling hills of the Sauerland. Their products are light and small, and are valuable relative to their weight, so that high freight costs do not constitute a particularly serious problem.

In the meanwhile a modern iron-smelting, steel-making, and steel-rolling industry grew up in the so-called Ruhr. In fact, however, very few industrial centres were located in the Ruhr valley. This was marginal to the coalfield. Iron-smelting grew up farther to the north, very roughly along the west–east axis of the little river Emscher. Here the coking coal was taken from the ground, and as fuel tended to be the most bulky of the raw material requirements of the industry, works were established as close as practicable to the coal mines. Small quantities of iron ore had formerly been available locally; it occurred interbedded with the coal, but this source was exhausted before the end of the nineteenth century, and the Ruhr area was obliged to rely on imported ore. This came from Scandinavia, from northern Spain, Italy, and North Africa. Almost all was brought in by sea, and works began to be established at sites near the coal mines, but at the same time easily accessible from the navigable waterways.

Fortunately the Ruhr area had the immense advantage of the river Rhine, which flowed across its western margin and provided a navigable highway down to the ocean port of Rotterdam. The Rhine tributaries in this area were of little commercial value, and were supplemented by canals. The Rhine-Herne Canal was constructed from the Rhine eastwards through the most industrialized part of the area (Figure 12). At its eastern terminus it linked with the Dortmund-Ems Canal, cut from the city of Dortmund northwards across the Plain to the navigable lower Ems river. At the mouth of the Ems the port of Emden handles imported ore, which it transfers to barges for the journey to the Ruhr.

Along this axis there grew up the most important industrial cities of the region: Duisburg and Ruhrort, at its western end, where the rivers Ruhr and Emscher and also the Rhine-Herne Canal join the Rhine; at Oberhausen, Essen, Gelsenkirchen, Bochum, and Dortmund. The smelting industry was, and still is, spread along this line, but its heaviest concentrations have come to be at the western and eastern ends, at Duisburg and Dortmund, because of the greater ease of handling the imported ore and of dispatching the heavy steel products from these points.

The Ruhr in the narrow sense does not have a particularly varied industrial structure. It is heavily dependent on iron and steel, though the by-products of the coke-ovens have given rise to some chemical manufactures, and the availability of heavy steel has led to the rise of constructional and engineering industries and most recently of the automobile industry in Bochum. But in the region which directly surrounds the Ruhr coalfield there is immense variety. A few miles to the south of the Ruhr valley is the narrow valley of the river Wupper. It is a small stream, flowing down to join the Rhine near Leverkusen, and at one time it provided water power to drive a few small woollen mills. Along its banks, in a situation reminiscent of Halifax or Rochdale, has grown up one of the more important textile and synthetic fibre manufacturing centres in West Germany, the city of Wuppertal. To the west of the Rhine is the cotton textile manufacturing centre of Mönchen-Gladbach and the silk and quality steel making city of Krefeld. To the north of the Ruhr, at Bielefeld, and out in the North German Plain near the Netherlands border, are other centres of the textile industry, notably Nordhorn, Gronau, and Bocholt. Many of these originated in small workshops which once processed the wool from the local sheep or wove the flax grown in the surrounding fields. Now they receive cotton or wool or jute through the port of Bremen, and weave it into fabrics.

The chemical industries are also of great importance in the North Rhine-Westphalian industrial area. Every battery of coke ovens is, in a sense, a chemical factory. The by-products of coke production include tar and gas. At some works the by-product separation is carried further and leads to the production of dyestuffs, fertilizers, and drugs.

At Leverkusen, on the Rhine between Cologne and Düsseldorf, is one of the larger chemical plants in West Germany, and at Cologne, Düsseldorf, and at several other cities in the area are factories producing either 'heavy' chemicals or the more refined products of the pharmaceutical, photographic, and dyestuffs industries. In recent years, oil refineries have been built in the vicinity of Cologne, at Dormagen, Wesseling, and Godorf. Crude oil is brought up the river by barge and now increasingly by pipeline from the ports. And all over the region are engineering industries: the building of Rhine barges, the preparation of constructional steel, the making of steel castings, and the assembling of complex pieces of machinery.

Hanover-Brunswick Region. About 140 miles to the north-east of the Ruhr is a younger, smaller, and less generalized industrial region. It centres in the cities of Hanover and Brunswick (Braunschweig). Both were ancient centres of craft industries. In recent years a fillip has been given to industrial development by the influx of refugees from the east. Here right up against the

Iron Curtain, many of them found employment in industries, established before the Second World War, but greatly expanded since. Foremost among these are the iron- and steel-works at Salzgitter-Watenstedt, established here in 1937 to use the low-grade iron ores of the vicinity, and at Peine. Northwest of Brunswick is Wolfsburg, where an automobile factory, planned before the Second World War, has since grown into the huge Volkswagen works. There are also a number of chemical engineering and light industries in the Brunswick region.

The Saarland. The remaining industrial regions lie south of the Central Uplands. Only the Saarland has its local source of coal, and the others are dependent on distant sources for their fuel and also for many of their industrial raw materials. The Saar industrial region is based almost exclusively on coal-mining, iron-smelting, steel-making, and engineering. Coal production is only about 16 million tons a year, and its quality is not particularly well suited to the needs of iron-smelting. It is, however, a good gas-coal, and is widely distributed in South Germany, but cannot compete in the export trade, except to eastern France, with the coal of the Ruhr. The steel industry of the Saarland is small compared with that of the Ruhr, and it is the only iron-smelting region in West Germany that at present relies heavily on French ores from Lorraine. Although the river Saar has been canalized within the industrial area, it is not yet possible to use water transport to communicate with the industrial regions of the Central and Lower Rhineland except through small and circuitous canals. The Saarland is more heavily dependent upon the railways than almost any other industrial region in the Federal Republic of Germany. The competitive position of the Saarland may be expected to improve with the completion of the Mosel canalization.

Rhine-Main Region. The northern part of the plain of the Upper Rhineland is highly industrialized. Like the North Rhine-Westphalian region, this was also an area of early urban development, where the German craft industries were developed to their highest level. Frankfurt and Mainz were among the largest cities of medieval Europe, and they remain today important centres of commerce and industry. The industrial structure of the Upper Rhineland provides an interesting contrast with that of the Lower Rhineland. It is farther from the ocean ports; it has no local sources of fuel, and most of the raw materials required by its industries have to be brought up the Rhine or southwards from the North Sea ports. A consequence of this is a very much greater concentration on light industries, which demand smaller quantities of materials, make heavier demands on labour, and require greater skill. The light machinery industry has long been relatively important here. Electrical and mechanical engineering, the more refined branches of the chemical industry, printing, and many forms of artwork play a large role in the industries of this region. But, like the Lower Rhineland, the Middle has also flowing through its midst the open thoroughfare of the river Rhine. Bulky and heavy materials can be freighted up the river and used at plants located along its banks. These, especially the heavy chemical industries of Höchst, Frankfurt, Wiesbaden, Mannheim, and Ludwigshafen, provide an exception to the generalization that the industries of South Germany are in general 'lighter' than those of the North.

Upper Rhine. The advantages of the Rhine-Main region are also shared by the Upper Rhineland industrial region. From the mouth of the Neckar to above Karlsruhe is an urbanized and industrialized region comparable with that around Frankfurt and Mainz. It is, however, a younger region. Speyer and Worms were great medieval cities, but the largest and most important, Mannheim, Ludwigshafen and Karlsruhe, grew up in modern times, and they owe their rise primarily to the river itself which bears their fuel and the raw materials of their chemical and engineering industries southward from the Lower Rhine region.

Swabia and Bavaria. The generalization that industries become 'lighter' with increasing distance from the coalfield is even more applicable to the rest of South Germany. This area is remote from the coalfields of the north and west, and only comparatively recently has it been linked with the Rhine by canals and canalized rivers large enough for modern needs. On the other hand, there is a long tradition of craftsmanship. Cottage industries and domestic crafts have furnished an historical background to the modern industries which require delicate manipulation and a fine sensitivity. The industries of this region are labour-intensive. The volume of their raw materials, as measured in tons, is relatively small; the number of man-hours of work expended on each unit of material is high. In the past it was clocks, mechanical toys, and dolls; now it is mechanical and electrical engineering, textile, and precision instruments. Amongst the foremost industries of South Germany is the manufacture of automobiles, especially at Unter-türkheim the home of Mercedes, Ingolstadt, Munich, and Heilbronn.

Three areas stand out on the map of South Germany. The first is the Neckar valley, with Stuttgart and Heilbronn as its chief centres. These cities are, however, surrounded by a number of smaller industrial towns, each dominated by a single important industry. The manufacture of automobiles and machinery is particularly important, and to these has been added in recent years one of the more important of the refugee industries from the Soviet Zone; the Zeiss factory for the manufacture of cameras and other types of precision equipment, which has been established at Oberkochen. Nuremberg also lies in the centre of a ring of smaller industrial cities which include Fürth and Erlangen. Engineering, both electrical and mechanical, is the dominant branch of industry, but food processing and printing industries and the manufacture of toys are also important. Like the Swabian industrial region, that of Nuremberg will also be linked with the Rhine by a navigable river when the Main-Danube project is completed. The Main, like the Neckar, has now been deepened and a series of dams and locks built to ease the problems of navigation. From

Nuremberg the small and now partly abandoned Ludwigskanal will be replaced by a larger canal link between the Main and Danube valleys.

Munich is the last of the major industrial centres of South Germany, with important electrical, optical, and food industries. It is the only one which does not have the advantage of water transport. The city lies on the Isar, a swift and variable stream that drops from its source in the Bavarian Alps to join the Danube. The Munich region stretches north-west to include Augsburg and Ulm. Its industries resemble in general those of the Nuremberg region. Engineering is prominent, especially in Augsburg, with the MAN works, but the emphasis is throughout also on those branches which require relatively small amounts of heavy or bulky raw materials.

These eight industrial regions account for most of West Germany's factory production. But scattered all over the country are industrial cities, large and small, in each of which some important branch of industry is to be found. Prominent among these is Kassel, in Hesse, with its engineering industries; Kassel is one of the most important German centres for the construction of railway locomotives, but it lies isolated and remote from other important centres. Schweinfurth, on the Main, is the chief German centre of the manufacture of ball-bearings. There is scarcely a single small German city without some factory or other: textile or leatherworking, engineering or the production of small items of apparel or of kitchen use.

To these industrial centres and industrial regions must be added West Berlin, juridically still the German capital. The sectors of the city of Berlin which were allocated to the Western Allies cover an area of 186 square miles. Before the war the city as a whole contained about 4·3 million people, and constituted one of the most important industrial areas in Germany. There were few types of manufacture that were not carried on here, but mechanical and electrical engineering dominated the industrial scene. Berlin's market covered most of central and eastern Germany. The eastern, or Soviet, sector

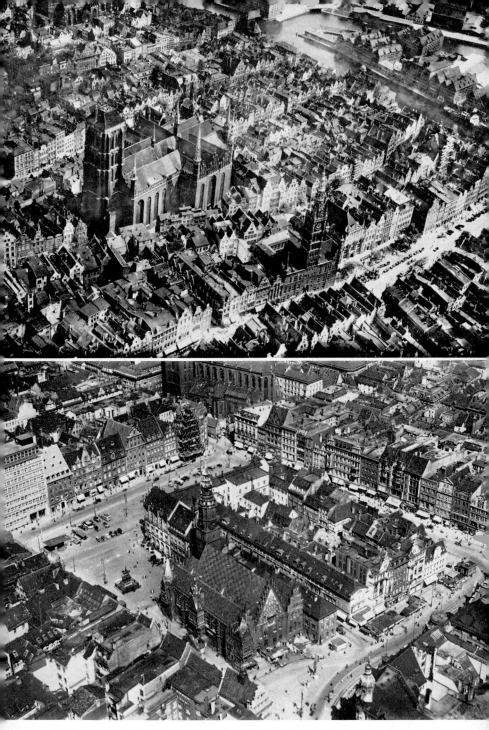

15. *Old Danzig, with the Motlau river, a branch of the Vistula, in the background. In the foreground is the Long Market (Langmarkt) with the Renaissance town hall (Rathaus). Behind it is the red brick, Gothic Marienkirche. A pre-war picture*

16. *The old town centre of Breslau; notice the large market square with the late medieval and Renaissance town hall. This is a pre-war picture; much of this part of Breslau has, however, been restored*

17. *The quaintness and beauty of the older German cities is unequalled. The buildings seen in this picture of Ochsenfurth, on the Main near Würzberg, belong (on the left) to the fifteenth and eighteenth centuries*

18. *Modern urban architecture: Nuremburg* (Nürnberg)

19. *The Walsum coalmine, on the western margin of the Ruhr coalfield, with thermal electric gencrating station and coal dock, opening off the Rhine*

20. *The small Waldenburg coalfield in Lower Silesia lies within the margin of the Sudeten mountains. It is more important for the coking quality of its coal than for the quantity produced*

21. *The Westfalenhülte iron and steel works at Dortmund*

continues to fulfil this role, but West Berlin is today an exclave of West Germany, isolated within the Soviet Zone. It has a population of about 2·25 million and contains within the limits of the city no resources that can be used industrially beyond small quantities of building materials. Agricultural land within the city is negligible; Berlin no longer serves as business and governmental centre for a large and powerful country. As a result of this structural change which has taken place in Berlin's economy 'the chief burden of future progress will fall upon industry'.* West Berlin's industries have had to expand far beyond their pre-war level in order to take the place formerly occupied by business and government service. This has been difficult. All fuel for industrial and domestic use has to be brought in, most of it from West Germany. The raw materials on which the industries operate have also to be imported from the West, and they must be paid for in exports to the West. This practice is maintained for political reasons; it would be cheaper, because transport charges would be less, to manufacture these commodities in West Germany. The industrial economy of West Berlin has then to be subsidized (see Chapter 6) in order to make it competitive with the industry of West Germany.

The industries now carried on in West Berlin tend to be those which lavish a great deal of labour on a small quantity of material. In this way the share of transport in the total production cost is minimized. With this qualification, West Berlin continues to pursue those branches of industry which had characterized it before the Second World War.

Over a quarter of the total employed persons (26 per cent in 1954) in West Berlin is employed directly in manufacturing industries, and a large number more who are employed in transport and commerce, are indirectly dependent on industry. Over half of the industrially employed are in mechanical (Borsig) and electrical (Siemens, AEG, and Osram) engineering.

* 'The Federal Republic of Germany', *Overseas Economic Surveys*, H.M.S.O., 1955, p. 309.

Next in importance come the clothing industries, especially DOB (Damenoberbekleidung), and, after them, food processing (Sarotti), printing (Ullstein), and the manufacture of chemicals (Schering).

Soviet-occupied Zone. Beyond the political boundaries of the Federal German Republic lie four other industrial regions which developed within the former territorial limits of Germany. They are Thuringia, Saxony, and Lausitz in the Soviet-occupied Zone and Central and Upper Silesia in the territory now administered by Poland. In addition there are, as in West Germany, a number of smaller industrial centres, each consisting of a single city and its immediate environs. Both the material basis and the types of specialization in most of these regions differ sharply from those in West Germany. Except in Upper Silesia, they are not based upon bituminous coal. Instead, the very extensive lignite deposits have been made not only a source of industrial power, but also of crude chemicals and even of coke for the blast furnace. The abundant and widely distributed reserves of potash and other salts have served as a basis for a chemical industry, and before the Second World War I. G. Farben had a great deal more than half its plant and equipment in what is today the Soviet-occupied Zone. Only in Upper Silesia, the so-called 'Eastern Ruhr', is there an industrial pattern closely similar to that of West Germany.

As a result of the division of Germany both the Federal Republic and the Soviet-occupied Zone were left without certain essential branches of industry. The Soviet Zone was relatively well off in chemicals, woollen textiles, and in thermal electric stations, operated with brown coal. Steel production was small and iron smelting negligible. Light and electrical engineering were well developed, but heavy engineering and a large number of specialized branches of the machinery industries were carried on mainly in the West. The authorities in the Soviet-occupied Zone have tried to remedy these deficiencies, generally at a high social cost, because the Zone does not present optimum conditions for these industries. A coke has been made from lignite, the so-called *Hochtemperaturbraun-kohlenkoks*; low blast furnaces have been designed to use it, and iron and steel works have been established at Stalinstadt, on the Oder, and at Calbe.

The industrial regions in both the Soviet Zone and the Polish-administered territory are based mainly upon the local resources in coal, lignite, and potash, and conform very approximately with the extent of these deposits.

Thuringia-Harz. Potash is the most important local resource, and it has given rise to some chemical industries. Formerly the hills which border this region were important for iron-working, and this industry, now defunct, has left a legacy of engineering works, among which the automobile plant at Eisenach and the Zeiss precision instrument works at Jena are important.

Saxony (Sachsen). The industrial region of Saxony is divisible into a more northerly part, lying in the plain and based upon the local reserves of lignite, and a more southerly, within the hills and deriving from the traditional craft industries of the region. Leipzig is the focus of the northern part, and around it is a ring of industrial centres, including Halle, Dessau, Merseburg, and Bitterfeld, in which the chemical industries are very strongly developed. The southern part of the region centres in Zwickau and Chemnitz, renamed Karl Marx-Stadt. Its chief industries, scattered through the valleys that open northwards from the Erzgebirge, are woollen textiles and mechanical engineering.

Nieder Lausitz. Brown coal is the most valuable and extensive fuel in the Soviet-occupied Zone, and the so-called East Elbian field is one of the largest and least used. The development plans of the Soviet Zone have called for an intensive development of this region. Lauchhammer, on its western margin, has become an important centre of mechanical engineering and chemical industries, for which the brown coal serves both as fuel and raw material. To the east, near Hoyerswerda, a new industrial combine, known as Schwarze Pumpe, has been established also on the basis of the brown coal resources.

Within the Soviet-occupied Zone of Germany are a number of smaller and more isolated centres of industry: Magdeburg, with its machine and chemical industries; Rostock, with its shipbuilding; Dresden, with electrical and mechanical engineering and chemical industries; East Berlin and its surrounding cities, Fürstenwalde, Potsdam, Brandenburg, and others, with their engineering and electrical, textile, clothing, and consumers' goods industries.

East Germany. The Upper Silesian industrial region is the largest and most important in the area now under Polish administration. The coalfield on which it is based is second only to that of the Ruhr in area and reserves, but it differs from that of the Ruhr in the presence of important ores of iron, lead, and zinc. Industry was developed here, largely by German initiative, in the late eighteenth century. During the nineteenth, when much of the coalfield area was under Prussian rule, it became an important source of coal, which was distributed over much of eastern Europe, of iron and later steel, and of lead and zinc.

Germany lost possession of much of the coalfield and industrial area after the First World War, and in 1945 the remainder also passed under Polish control. The coalfield and industrial region of Upper Silesia had become important in the economy of eastern Germany and of the territories lying farther to the east. It had in part supplied Berlin with fuel and its engineering industries with metal.

In addition to the large industrial complex of Upper Silesia, East Germany contains also several small and more isolated industrial centres. These include the small Lower Silesian or Waldenburg coalfield, the city of Breslau (Wrocław), with its engineering industries, and the city of Stettin (Szczecin), with its ship-building and port industries.

These industries lying east of the Iron Curtain were formerly integrated, both in their organization and control and by the exchange of their specialized products, with those of West Germany. Today there is virtually no contact between them.

The industries of the Federal German Republic are gradually being fitted into a West European pattern; those of Central and East Germany are being integrated by means of coordinated development plans into the industrial pattern of the Communist *bloc* (see p. 125).

West Germany today contains about 12·5 million refugees (see above, p. 8). The majority have been absorbed into industry, and a few have brought their industrial employment with them, thus making a direct contribution to the economy of the Federal Republic. It is impossible to form a precise estimate of the number of enterprises which owe their origin to the refugees. By September 1950, it has been claimed, 'a total of 85,127 fugitive business establishments of all types had been set up in West Germany'. Most, of course, were very small, and many failed to survive for long, but a few were transferred from Central and East Germany almost as operating concerns. Foremost among these is the Carl Zeiss plant of Jena, producer of cameras and of the highest quality precision instruments. Many of its workers and much of its equipment were shifted from Jena to the west, before the Russians were able to get their hands on them, and were established at Oberkochen. There are other instances of bodies of workers, able to bring only their skills with them, who reassembled in the west and reformed and recapitalized their former industrial undertaking. When once the immediate problems of adjustment and assimilation had been faced, the refugees began to play an important role in certain branches of West German industry. Nearly a third of the textile workers, it has been claimed, are refugees from the Soviet Zone, the Polish-administered eastern provinces, and the Sudetenland; most of the makers of porcelain and ceramics, glass and costume jewellery are from the Sudetenland. Any consideration of the immensely rapid increase in industrial production in the Federal Republic should not fail to add that the economy has gained immeasurably at the expense of the Soviet Zone, the eastern provinces, and the Sudetenland by the influx of refugee industries.

We have already surveyed the regional distribution of industry in Germany. Let us turn to a short examination of three major branches of industry.

Iron, Steel, and Engineering Industries

'The foundations of the modern industrial state of Germany,' wrote the author of a British report on the German economy, 'stand upon the bedrock of a powerful coal and steel industry.' These industries before the war showed a high degree of concentration. Steel was dominated by only six concerns, and these had developed a vertical structure of control which reached from iron ore and coal-mining to automobile factory and shipyard. This concentration of industrial power was broken up after the Second World War, and its redevelopment has been resisted by the Federal Government. The iron and steel industries do not seem to have suffered in the process. Output has increased continuously. In 1952, when the Federal Republic joined the Coal and Steel Community, all controls on output were removed, and production has continued to soar:

	Pig Iron	Crude Steel	Rolled Steel Goods
1950	9,806	13,116	9,148
1952	13,527	17,699	12,375
1954	13,815	19,778	13,549
1956	17,577	23,189	17,813
1957	18,358	24,507	18,897
1958	16,659	22,785	17,420
1959	18,393	25,824	19,360
1960	25,739	34,100	25,841

(in millions of metric tons)

The steel production of the Federal Republic is today (1960) the third largest in the world, and is exceeded only by the United States and the Soviet Union. Despite the loss of the small steel industry in the Soviet-occupied Zone and the larger industry of Upper Silesia, the West German iron and steel industry is now 50 per cent greater than that of the whole of

Germany before the Second World War. Plants dismantled in the late 1940s have been replaced, and many of the older works have been modernized. The greater part of the capacity, about 85 per cent, is in the Ruhr, where it has the advantages of local fuel and good transport facilities. Other important centres are the Saarland, Lübeck, Salzgitter, and Peine, close to Hanover. A plant has recently been built on the Weser below Bremen in order to smelt imported ore. The only other places where the iron and steel industry is carried on are around Siegen in the Siegerland, and at Amberg in northern Bavaria. In both these areas the industry is a direct descendant of the ancient charcoal-iron industry, established first in these hills because of the abundance of timber to be found there and the existence of local ores. Their scale of operation is today very small.

Germany relies heavily on imported ore. The domestic ores are mostly low-grade, and the economies to be had from the use of a high-grade ore are sufficient to offset the greater freight charges. The present trend is to use ever smaller quantities of domestic ores, except at the Salzgitter and Peine furnaces which are built on or close to the ore-field.

The steel furnace charge normally contains a high proportion of scrap. A highly developed economy like Germany's, generates a great deal of scrap, much of which is fed back to the steel furnaces. A large part—about 50 per cent in 1960—of the steel production is made in the open hearth. Only about 40 per cent is made in the converter, which yields a poorer quality metal. Germany was a pioneer in the manufacture of high-grade steel in the electric furnace, and this branch of steel production remains of very great importance, yielding about 7 per cent of the total steel production. The chief centre for the manufacture of high quality steel is the Deutsche Edelstahlwerke A.G. at Krefeld.

Rolled goods, especially steel bars, heavy plate and thin sheet and strip make up the chief products of the steel works, and constitute the raw material of the engineering industries. It is impossible to generalize about this latter branch of German manufactures. It is carried on in an immense number of factories and workshops. In 1960 there were over 12,000 firms which employed more than ten persons. There were probably far more metal-using firms which fell below this size limit. Almost half the engineering firms lay in North Rhine-Westphalia, where the supply of their raw material was easiest and the market for their product was largest. But, as has already been seen, the engineering industry is very widespread, with those works which make the more intensive use of the metal being found, in general, farther from the source of supply. The manufacture of machine tools and of ball-bearings, both highly important branches of the engineering industry, is carried on mainly in South Germany. Automobile manufacture is very widely distributed. Wolfsburg, Düsseldorf, and Hanover are important centres in North Germany, and an automobile factory has recently been established at Bochum; Stuttgart, Ulm, Heilbronn, Munich, Rüsselsheim (near Mainz), Ingolstadt, Dingolfing, Untertürkheim, and Nuremberg are among the chief centres of automobile and tractor manufacture in the south. Kassel, with the Henschel works, make automobiles as well as railway locomotives; and Lübeck builds dredgers. Heavy mining, earth-moving, and dredging equipment is made in the mining areas, notably by Krupp in Essen and Phönix-Rheinruhr in Duisburg-Ruhrort. Constructional steel is prepared from rolled steel 'profiles' mainly in the Ruhr; nuts and bolts, wire and nails are made in a multitude of small factories, many of them in the Sauerland, and all over West Germany are small factories which press, stamp, and forge either small articles of everyday use or the components of larger machines. In Württemberg, in particular, small components are made for the machines and equipment built in the larger industrial centres.

Electrical engineering is more widely and more evenly distributed than mechanical, in part because the input of materials is smaller and that of labour proportionally greater. This branch of industry suffered very severely from war-time destruction and post-war dismantling. Berlin was the most important centre of the electrical engineering industry, but suffered very severely during and after the war. Electrical engineering remains an important industry in West Berlin, but there has been an important shift to West Germany. The chief factories of Siemens-Halske and Siemens-Schuckert, for example, are now no longer in Berlin, but respectively Munich and Erlangen. The radio industry is now concentrated in Fürth, with the Grundig factories, and at Villigen in the Black Forest. Electric lamps are made at Aachen and at Neheim-Hüsten in Westphalia.

The shipbuilding industry is a heavy consumer of the products of the steel and engineering industries. For the first five years after the war German shipbuilding was limited to fishing and other very small craft. In 1951 all controls on shipbuilding were removed, and the industry very quickly recovered; in size it is now second only to that of Great Britain in Europe. German shipbuilding yards, located mainly in Hamburg, Bremen, and Kiel, are noteworthy for the extreme speed of their construction. Among the vessels built in recent years at German yards have been a number of the giant supertankers.

The Chemical Industry

The chemical industry was before the war one of the most highly developed in Germany, and contributed on a large and important scale to Germany's export trade. No less than about 85 per cent of it was controlled in one way or another by I. G. Farben (Interessengemeinschaft Farbenindustrie A.G.), which thus constituted one of the most formidable of the concentrations of economic power. The chemical industry was relatively more important in eastern Germany than in western. No less than 55 per cent, it has been estimated, of the total I. G. Farben assets lay in what is now the Soviet Zone of Germany. This is largely to be accounted for by the naturally occurring deposits of potash and common salt, and of the lignite which was used extensively in the chemical industry. A consequence of this has been that the Federal Republic has had to expand its chemical production relatively more than many other branches of industry as a result of the division of Germany.

The largest chemical works in West Germany were formerly part of the immense I. G. Farben. This concern has been broken up into a small number of more specialized firms. Largest of these are the Leverkusen works of Farbenfabrik Bayer A.G., which spreads along the right bank of the Rhine between Cologne and Düsseldorf, and the Ludwigshafen works of the Badische Anilin- und Soda-Fabrik A.G., lying across the Rhine from Mannheim. Other important chemical works are at Frankfurt and Höchst, in the Rhine-Main region; a plant at Duisburg, which is engaged primarily in processing the metalliferous residues of other chemical processes, and the Hüls works, lying to the north of the Ruhr, which is concerned mainly in the manufacture of synthetic rubber.

This small number of very large works accounts today for the greater part of the present production of chemicals, both the heavy or basic chemicals and also the synthetic fibres, dye-stuffs, and pharmaceutical products. A few small and more specialized factories are to be found, notably those engaged in the production of high explosives, such as the Dynamit-AG, at Troisdorf, near Bonn, and, of course, every major coke-oven plant in the Ruhr or Saarland is itself a producer of certain heavy chemicals, such as ammonia, sulphuric acid, tar, benzol, and other by-products, and every steelworks that uses the basic process turns out superphosphate for agriculture. The rubber industry, which is also in some measure a chemical industry, is carried on mainly at Hamburg, Hanover, Fulda, and in and around Frankfurt.

The Textile and Clothing Industries

The textile industry of Germany was never, like that of Great Britain, concentrated on or near the coalfields. This was, in part at least, because the railways had come into existence to distribute fuel before most of the scattered mills had gone over to the use of mechanical power. The Soviet Zone and the territories now under Polish administration contained a relatively large share of the textile industries. If generalization is possible, it may be said that the woollen industry predominated in the east, while cotton-spinning and weaving were more widely distributed in the west. This pattern of distribution accords with the general availability of materials. The cotton industry, a more recent one than the age-old manufacture of woollens, is carried on in fairly large mills; it dominates the industrial scene in Mönchen-Gladbach and Wuppertal, and is important in Bremen, in the small industrial cities along the Netherlands border, and at several places in South Germany. The textile industries, as a whole, are heavy employers of female labour, and thus are in some degree complementary to the engineering industries, in such cities as Bremen and Hanover in which employment is heavily male. The woollen weaving and spinning industries had been carried on in East Germany and in cities of South Germany, mainly in small establishments. A great many of these were disrupted by the Russian invasion, and in some instances management and workers migrated to the West, where they play a very important role in the textile industry of the Federal Republic.

The natural silk industry of Germany is carried on mainly in the Lower Rhineland. Krefeld has long been its centre, but it has spread also to the neighbouring cities of Mönchen-Gladbach and Rheydt, and also to Wuppertal and Bielefeld. Jute manufacture, using materials imported mainly from Pakistan, is also concentrated in North Germany, and the largest mill is in the port of Hamburg.

The German textile industry has recovered since the war less rapidly and less completely than most others. This is in part to be explained in terms of changes in consumers' demands—the greater interest in cars, television, and other durable consumers' goods—in part also of the competition of imported fabrics and domestically produced synthetic fibres.

The manufacture of synthetic fibres had been well developed

before the war, partly as a result of the drive to attain self-sufficiency. Almost half the plant lay in eastern Germany. The acute shortage of silk stockings in West Germany after the war was due to the fact that the manufacturing centres lay mainly in the Soviet-occupied Zone. This loss to the West German consumer has been compensated by the post-war expansion of the chemical factories—and also of the hosiery mills—in the Federal Republic.

The German leather footwear industry has followed the fortunes of the textile, and has, in fact, barely regained its pre-war level of production. Leather footwear is meeting with increasing competition from that made of rubber and synthetic materials, and demand has contracted. The chief centres of the industry are at Pirmasens in the Pfalz, at Stuttgart, and the small near-by city of Weinheim, and at Offenbach and Worms in the Middle and Upper Rhineland.

The paper industry was heavily concentrated in the east, and heavy investment has been necessary to equip West Germany to satisfy its needs. North Rhine-Westphalia, the Upper Rhineland, and the Bavarian Forest are now the chief areas for the production of paper, cardboard, and related materials.

The ceramics and glass industries are very widely distributed. A relatively large proportion lies in eastern Germany, which is richer in the raw materials of these industries. But the western industries suffered little destruction during the war—apart from the manufacture of sanitary ware, which was chiefly carried on in North Rhine-Westphalia and has been reinforced by the immigration of glass and ceramic workers, chiefly from the Sudetenland. Glass is today made in Essen and Düsseldorf and in many small factories, which are particularly numerous in the hills of northern Bavaria.

Industrial Growth

German industrial growth during the past dozen years has been spectacular; it has also been uneven as between its several branches. There are very few industries that do not show a considerable expansion above their highest level of the pre-war years, and in some branches of industry, notably electrical and mechanical engineering and the chemical industries, this growth has been truly spectacular. To some extent, of course, this growth is not only explained but also made necessary by the growth in population. The population of the Federal Republic is today 34 per cent greater than in the corresponding area in 1938. Industrial growth in the Federal Republic is, however, proportionately much greater than this. The following table, adapted from the *Statistisches Jahrbuch* of the Federal Republic (1961) shows the amount of growth in the major sectors of industry during the past six years.

	Mining	Energy	Iron & Steel	Chemicals	Total Industry
1954	128	158	141	158	155
1956	143	197	193	196	192
1958	147	216	184	236	209
1960	146	260	242	308	249
		(1950=100)			

Discrepancies between the sectors are explained, as has already been indicated in part by changes in consumer choice: the growth of synthetic fibre at the expense of natural, and of rubber at the expense of leather. A more significant factor, however, has been the division of Germany with, initially at least, a preponderance of the chemical, electric power generation, ceramic, and woollen textile industries in the Soviet Zone, and of coal-mining, iron-, and steel-making and of mechanical construction and cotton textile industries in the Federal Republic. An uneven industrial growth was necessitated by the nature of the partition of Germany. Both the Federal Republic and the Soviet Zone have greatly expanded their industrial potential in order to provide themselves with those branches of industry of which they were deprived by the fact of the division of the country.

In the previous chapter we considered briefly the proportion of the working population engaged in agriculture and the contribution of agriculture to the gross national product. It was suggested that, in relation to its input of labour and materials, West German agriculture is relatively inefficient. Not so West German manufacturing industries. The following table* shows the contribution of the main sectors of the West German economy to the total national income:

	1950	1956	1960
Basic Industries	22,485	56,451	77,871
of which mining and quarrying	2,173	5,260	7,297
iron and steel	4,350	13,595	16,958
chemical	6,783	14,661	22,267
Investment Goods	18,253	55,400	84,140
Consumers' Goods	20,336	36,764	47,269
of which textiles	9,838	14,388	16,364
Others	19,321	37,031	44,395
Total	80,395	185,646	253,675

(in millions of DM)

Industry and mining together constitute the fastest growing sector of the German economy. In 1950 it contributed 45·8 per cent of the gross national product, and in 1960, 53·6 per cent. The productivity of West German labour is relatively high, and unquestionably the Federal Republic of Germany is making better use of its resources in labour and materials than is the Soviet Zone. In the last chapter we shall return to Germany's competitive position in the European economy. Let us turn now to Germany's transport, communications, and trade, which together make up the second largest sector of the economy.

* Source: *Leistung in Zahlen, 1961–62*, Bundesministerium fur Wirtschaft, Bonn, 1962.

Transport and Communications

The widespread, thriving industry, described in the last chapter, is dependent upon one of the most highly developed systems of transport and communication in the world. The construction of this system was begun early, and, despite the political fragmentation of Germany throughout much of the nineteenth century, it had very largely been completed by its end. This was due, in part, to the enlightened policy pursued by some of the German states, in part to intensive publicity for railways which had been staged by a number of prominent industrialists and business men. Foremost among these was Friedrich List, who, two years before the first short length of railway was opened, gave the public an accurate prognosis of the layout of the future railway system and an appraisal of its advantages.

The first German railway was opened in 1835 in Bavaria; it was the short stretch from Nuremberg to Fürth, about five miles. A few years only sufficed to break down the resistance of the conservative and the incredulous. The 1840s and 1850s were a period of rapid railway building. Berlin began slowly to shape up as the focus of the German system, as List had prophesied that it would. By 1850—that is, within a period of only fifteen years—3,000 miles of railway had been laid down within the German borders as they were then established. Despite the political divisions, more through routes were constructed in Germany than in highly unified France.

The effect of this railway system was revolutionary. 'It was the railways', wrote Treitschke, 'which first dragged the nation from its economic stagnation; they completed what the Zoll-verein had only begun; with such power did they break in upon all the old habits of life, that already in the forties the aspect of Germany was completely changed.' A network of railways was made to radiate from Berlin. The most important and most used lines were those running in a generally westerly direction from Berlin to Hamburg, through Hanover to the Rhineland, and south-westward from Berlin through Saxony and Thuringia and into Bavaria. Another highly important group of railway lines followed the Rhine valley from the Ruhr area upstream to Frankfurt and Mannheim, and from there connected south-eastward with Bavaria. Around and between these trunk lines there developed a network of lines more of local than of national importance. Taken together, these gave Germany one of the densest rail networks of any country in Europe during the nineteenth century.

The division of Germany truncated these lines. The use of a number of lines has had to be discontinued at the Iron Curtain, as the diminished rail traffic between the Federal Republic and the Soviet Zone is at present restricted to only three routes. The use of German railways has been given a new orientation. In the past the traffic flow was, apart from the north–south movement along the Rhine valley, in the main from east to west or north-east to south-west. Of necessity, it is now more from north to south, and the most intensively used section of the Federal railway system is that which joins the North Sea ports and the North Rhine-Westphalian, Upper Rhine, and Bavarian centres of industry and population.

The German railway system owed its origin to a combination of private and State enterprise; the many sections were later merged into a State-operated system. Today the Federal Railway (*Bundesbahn*) is managed by a directorate appointed by the Transport Minister, and for convenience of administration is divided into sixteen divisions, or *Bundesbahndirektionen*, not unlike the division of British Railways into its several Regions. The *Bundesbahn* is one of the most efficient and effective systems in the world. No traveller on the German railway can fail to

22. *The Volkswagen works at Wolfsburg. To the left is the Mittelland Canal which provides transport for bulky goods*

23. *The Bayer chemical and dyestuffs factory at Leverkusen, between Cologne and Düsseldorf. On the upper left-hand corner of the photograph is the river Rhine, used for transporting many bulky commodities to the factory*

24. *This new superhighway leads up to the new Severin Bridge (Severinsbrücke) across the Rhine at Cologne*

25. *Frankfurt-on-Main: the main railway station lies close to the river Main. In the middle distance is the rebuilt 'Old City' with the tower of the cathedral*

26. *The Rhein-Main airport at Frankfurt-on-Main is almost encircled by the multi-lane road of the Autobahn system. Here at the Frankfurter Kreuz, the Autobahn from N.W. Germany to Nuremberg crosses that from Hanover to Karlsruhe*

27. *The port of Hamburg is not only the oldest but by far the most important in West Germany. In the middle distance is the Elbe river, with the old city and the Alster Lake beyond*

28. *The Duisburg-Ruhrort docks lie where the river Ruhr (top right, closed by a sluice) enters the Rhine. The docks handle chiefly coal and iron-ore*

envy the cleanliness and the punctuality of the service or to appreciate such little attentions to the convenience of travellers as the plan of the coaches which is often exhibited on the platforms of the larger stations. The German railways have relied very heavily on steam traction, and have been slower in converting to electricity or diesel propulsion than several other countries of Western Europe. Recently the task has been completed of electrifying the trunk lines from Basel along the Rhine to Cologne, and north-east to Hamburg and south-east to Nuremberg, Munich, and the Austrian border. Several lines in the Ruhr, the Saar, and in Baden-Württemberg have also been electrified, and it is planned to electrify all main lines in the country.

The more rapid acceleration of electric locomotives, quite apart from their greater cleanliness, will give great advantages over steam on routes which are used intensively.

Rivers and Canals

The development of railways was long preceded by the use of the rivers. Roman bas-reliefs record the conveyance of wine and other commodities by rowing-boats along the Mosel and Rhine. All through the Middle Ages the rivers provided the most used avenue of transport and communications. Long-distance commerce moved up and down the Rhine between Basel and ports in the Low Countries; lumber was rafted down the small rivers from the hills, and almost every stream large enough to float a boat was used to carry farm products to the neighbouring market-towns. The river-borne traffic led to the growth of commercial cities along the banks. It also led to the imposition of burdensome and unnecessary tolls. At one time a cargo moving down the Rhine had to pay a toll at no less than about thirty stations, and the sum of the tolls often exceeded the initial value of the cargo. This was a major factor in the decline of the use of the Rhine and also of other rivers in the later Middle Ages. The romantically placed castles, which decorate the steep valley sides of the Rhine gorge, were put there, not for the delight of the modern tourist, but to enforce the collection of tolls from passing ships.

These burdensome tolls were not abolished until the Rhineland was invaded and conquered by the French in the Revolutionary wars. During the nineteenth century much was done to improve conditions on the river. At various points the channel was deepened by blasting away the bedrock; at others the course of the river was straightened and its flow made more regular. In 1816 the first steam-driven boat sailed on the Rhine. During the following years the volume of traffic steadily increased, and the Rhine began again to assume the role that it had played during the Middle Ages. After the middle of the nineteenth century iron ore and coal, carried respectively to and from the Ruhr industrial region, began to make up a large part of the freight. Some of the early South German railways were tributary to the river, designed to deliver materials to the points where the barges loaded or to distribute the goods brought up the river. But already, by the middle of the century, a start had been made on improving the tributaries of the Rhine and making them more easily navigable. From Strasbourg, which remained French until 1871, a canal was cut around the northern end of the High Vosges, to cross Lorraine and join up with the river Marne and the other rivers which converge on Paris. The Main was improved so that barges might sail right up to Frankfurt instead of transhipping their cargoes in Mainz.

Other German rivers also attained a considerable importance in Germany's internal trade. The Weser, Aller, Elbe, and Oder were all used, not only during the Middle Ages, but also in the nineteenth and twentieth centuries. These rivers all flowed roughly from south to north, or south-east to north-west, and entered the North or Baltic Sea. During the late nineteenth century the most urgent demand was for transport facilities in a west to east direction, across the northern plain. This was in part supplied by the construction of the northern system of railways, but the advantages of river and canal transport were such as to lead to the construction of a system of artificial

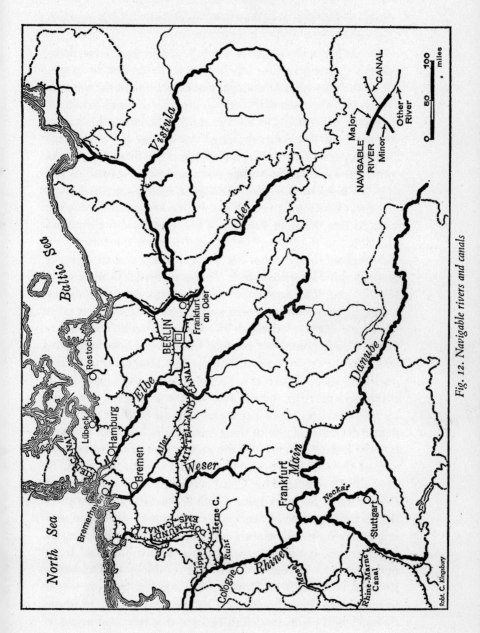

Fig. 12. Navigable rivers and canals

waterways to link together and supplement the northward flowing rivers.

We have seen already how naturally suited was the northern plain to the construction of canals. The damp marshy tracts, left by the post-glacial drainage, join the valleys of the present-day rivers. They required little grading, and canals could be excavated with ease. The earliest canal to be cut in this region was the Elbe-Trave Canal, across the base of the Schleswig-Holstein peninsula between the Elbe and the Baltic Sea. It was constructed during the Middle Ages, and, though small, is still used. Its modern successor, the Kiel Canal, is discussed later. The first of the modern canals were those of the Ruhr industrial area. At first the river Ruhr itself had been used for shipping coal down to the Rhine, but it ceased to serve this function as the more southerly mines became exhausted and the mining industry shifted northwards. It remains navigable, however, up to Mülheim. This northward spread of mining and industry led to the construction of two canals, each of which runs from the Rhine eastward through the industrial area. The Rhine-Herne Canal, completed in 1914, follows the Emscher valley and links the most important of the coal mines and iron- and steel-works (see Figure 12). To the north is the Lippe Canal, completed in 1930, which follows the course of the river Lippe, and skirts the northern margin of the coalfield. But even before the construction of these canals, steps had been taken to link the industrial centres in the eastern part of the Ruhr area, around the city of Dortmund, with the North Sea ports. In 1899 the Dortmund-Ems Canal was opened from the city of Dortmund to the river Ems, which flows northwards to enter the sea near the port of Emden. Emden at once developed into one of the most important German ports for the handling of bulk cargoes. It thus became possible to distribute coal from both the western extremity of the coalfield at Duisburg-Ruhrort, and also from Dortmund at the east. Iron ore began to move into the industrial area by the same routes, and new iron and steel plants tended to be located as near as possible to those western and eastern ports of entry into the Ruhr industrial region. The Lippe and Rhine-Herne canals served to distribute industrial raw materials and products between these two all-important terminal facilities.

The next step was to link this growing network of canals in Westphalia eastwards with the Weser and Elbe rivers. This was achieved by the larger, longer, and more ambitious Mittelland Canal. At its western end it joined the Dortmund-Ems Canal, and was thus connected with the Ruhr. Eastwards, it passed near Osnabrück, Minden, where it crossed the Weser, Hanover, Brunswick, and Magdeburg, where it joined the Elbe. From the Elbe, a few miles below Magdeburg, the Elbe-Havel Canal was extended eastwards to join the network of canals that permeated and encircled Berlin and stretched eastwards to the Oder and the Vistula.

These canals, together with the rivers which they interconnected, were modern in concept and design. They were intended to carry barges of over a thousand tons; they were built as straight as the terrain permitted, and their banks were strengthened to prevent them from being damaged by the wash of fast, powered barges.

A similar network of waterways is in process of construction to link the Upper Rhine with neighbouring river basins. The Main has now been made navigable for barges of over a thousand tons as far upstream as Bamberg, and the Neckar to above Stuttgart. The idea of linking the Rhine basin, by way of the Main, with the Danube, is very far from new. A small —by modern standards uneconomically small—canal was cut by King Ludwig II of Bavaria from near Nuremberg to the Danube above Regensburg. It is still shown on the map as the Ludwigskanal, and is sometimes used by those curious people who set out to cross Europe by canoe and canal; but it is partly dry and has no commercial significance. A modern canal, with a similar capacity to that of the river Main, is now under construction, and by 1970 should provide an effective waterway between the Main and Danube.

On the other side of the Rhine is the drainage basin of the Meuse and of the rivers which flow to join the Seine near Paris. A similar link with these river systems has long been planned. Early in the nineteenth century, as we have already seen, a canal was cut from the Rhine near Strasbourg to join the Upper Meuse and Marne. A branch from this canal links it with the river Saar and the Saarland industrial region. These canals are small, and are less intensively used than those which radiate from the Lower Rhineland. Of potentially greater importance is the Mosel. This river, which rises on the western flanks of the Vosges, flows northwards through the French province of Lorraine before curving gently towards the north-east, crossing the Rhine plateau, and joining the Rhine itself at Coblenz. In its upper course the Mosel is joined by canals with the Meuse and the Paris river system, and also southwards to the Saône and Rhône. The linking canals are small, but could be enlarged, and their potential importance is considerable. The problem has always lain in the lower course of the Mosel, where the deeply incised valley of this river cuts across the Rhineland plateau. The river here is slow-flowing and meandering; its bed is deeply silted; it is navigable only for small vessels, and has, in fact, not been used commercially for many centuries.

The potential importance of the Mosel lies largely in the fact that it links Lorraine, which contains the largest reserves of iron ore in Western Europe, with the Rhineland in which occurs the most important coalfield in Western Europe. If the Mosel had been as easily navigated as the Rhine or Elbe, it is possible that an interdependence of these two important resources might have arisen as the industries themselves developed. This, however, did not happen. The Ruhr came to depend mainly on imported ores that were transhipped in Rotterdam or Emden and were freighted up the rivers and canals to the ironworks. Many times during the later nineteenth century and early in the present century, the canalization of the Mosel was suggested. But always it was opposed either by the political rivalries of France and Germany, or by the vested interests of industrialists who had become wedded to the existing pattern of trade and saw no reason for change. Broadly speaking, it was the Lorraine interests that demanded the canalization and improvement of the Mosel, seeing it as a means of cheapening and facilitating their fuel supply. In general, it was the Ruhr concerns which had adjusted their plant to higher grade imported ores and saw no reason to benefit their rivals in Lorraine, and the railways, which foresaw a loss of freight, that opposed the project most strongly.

The river Saar is a small, navigable tributary of the Mosel. The iron and steel industry which grew up along its valley used the local coal, despite its indifferent quality, to smelt iron ore brought by rail across from the Lorraine orefield, only some thirty miles away. The navigable Saar was of some importance for transport within the Saarland industrial region itself, and it was linked by the Saar Coal Canal with the Rhine-Marne Canal, but the water connection direct with the Mosel and Rhine was scarcely used at all. The Saar coalfield has long had close contacts with Lorraine, and the interdependence of the two regions dates from at least as far back as the middle of the nineteenth century. After the First World War, the Saar mines were held by the French for a period of fifteen years, and after the Second World War the area was, in effect, detached from the French-occupied Zone of Germany and incorporated into France. In 1956 an agreement was reached between France and the Federal Government whereby the Saarland was restored to West Germany, while the Federal Government undertook to facilitate the canalization of the Mosel. Plans have been prepared, work has been begun, and it is anticipated that, by the end of 1963, barges, loaded with coal in the docks of Ruhrort, will carry their cargoes direct to the ironworks near Thionville and Metz, and return with Lorraine ore for the Ruhr furnaces. So simple a pattern of transport as this requires something more than careful planning; it demands the retooling of much of the Ruhr industry before ores of such radically different grade and quality can be used.

Before the Second World War Germany's inland waterways carried about 30 per cent of her total internal freight, and a very much larger proportion of all bulky and heavy goods. The waterways suffered severely from the bombing. In many instances their bridges and locks were the direct objectives of attack. The barge fleets were sunk and collapsed bridges blocked the waterways. The canals have now been entirely restored, the fleet of barges rebuilt, and the part played by water-borne transport is now greater, both relatively and absolutely than before the war. The division of Germany has, however, altered the pattern of river and canal transport, just as it has that of rail. The importance of west–east transport has been diminished, and that of north–south increased. The Mittelland Canal and its eastward continuations still constitute one of the recognized means of access to West Berlin, but the traffic on the canal between Brunswick and Magdeburg and that on the Elbe above Hamburg are very greatly diminished. It is no longer possible for barges to reach the port of Hamburg from Northwest Germany by going east along the Mittelland Canal and down the Elbe. On the other hand, the Rhine and its navigable tributaries are more important than ever before, and an entirely new canal has been proposed from the Lower Elbe and the port of Hamburg southwards to the Mittelland Canal. Within the Russian-occupied Zone, most of which had formerly been served by the port of Hamburg, a canal is now projected from the Havel northwards to the port of Rostock.

This recent development of water-borne transport has been in some measure at the expense of the railways. The movement of goods by water is cheaper than by rail, and modern factories —at least those handling bulky raw materials—have tended to locate themselves close to navigable waterways. The German railways had long opposed the canalization of the Mosel, which would compete with them in the handling of bulk materials between the Rhineland, the Saar, and Lorraine. Now both railway and waterway are being threatened by the competition first of road transport and most recently of pipelines, laid down from the northern parts to oil refineries along the Rhine.

Ports of the Federal Republic

The German North Sea ports gained an immense advantage from the orientation of German rivers. These flowed from south-east to north-west, and thus extended the hinterlands served by the ports at their mouths and reached by barge traffic to cover much of Central Europe.

The hinterland of Hamburg, that is the area which could be reached by barge from its port, stretched over most of what is now the Soviet Zone and the eastern provinces now under Polish administration, as well as much of Czechoslovakia. Hamburg is now cut off from most of this hinterland, and the Soviet Zone has been left without a major ocean port. At present the formerly minor port of Rostock is being developed and extended to serve the needs of the Soviet Zone. Meanwhile the Federal Republic has the major ports of Hamburg and Bremen, and the minor ports of Kiel, Lübeck, and Emden. The volume of traffic handled by each of these in 1960 was:

	Exports	Imports	Total Trade
Hamburg	7,788·8	22,965·5	30,754·3
Bremen	5,377·3	8,018·4	13,395·7
Emden	2,064·7	8,205·2	10,269·9
Lübeck	776·5	2,261·1	3,037·6
Kiel	44·9	872·6	917·5

(in thousands of metric tons)

Hamburg and Bremen are general ports, handling the widest possible range of commodities. Both have developed what are commonly termed the 'port industries' as well as handling the export and import trade of the industrial regions lying to the south. Both have outports in Cuxhaven and Bremerhaven respectively, at which ships call to unload or load part cargoes, which do not justify the voyage up-river to Hamburg or Bremen.

Emden is more specialized. Its canal connection with the Ruhr gives it an important role in handling iron ore and coal. Lübeck and Kiel serve as commercial ports only for the small area in the extreme north-east of the Federal Republic, and neither is particularly well placed or well equipped. Lübeck, however, carries on an important passenger traffic with Sweden and Finland. Kiel was in origin a naval port, and was the chief base of the German fleet. The Kiel Canal, which cuts across the Schleswig-Holstein peninsula and links Kiel with the North Sea, was originally built and opened in 1895 in order to allow the German fleet an unobtrusive access to the North Sea from the security of its bases on the Baltic. It was internationalized after the First World War, and is now again open to any peaceful commerce that wishes to eliminate the long voyage around the north of Denmark. The direct import of crude oil is mainly through Hamburg, Emden, and its neighbour Wilhelmshaven, from which it is distributed, in part by pipe-line, to refineries in the Rhineland.

Among the most important of the ports which serve the Federal Republic are those which have grown up at or near the Rhine mouths, in the Netherlands and Belgium. Foremost among these is Rotterdam. A significant part of its traffic is made up of coal exported from the Ruhr and the bulky imports of the Ruhr and Rhineland. Dock facilities have been built for the rapid transhipment of coal, iron ore, lumber, and grain from river-barge to ocean-going freighter and vice versa, and a new port, Europort, is being developed to the west of Rotterdam to help handle this growing international traffic. The ports of Amsterdam and Antwerp play a similar part, but their share of this traffic is smaller, mainly because of their greater distance from the main navigable channel of the river Rhine and the increased navigational difficulties in reaching them.

The German Road System

During the period of intensive development of railway, river and canal transport, the roads were somewhat neglected.

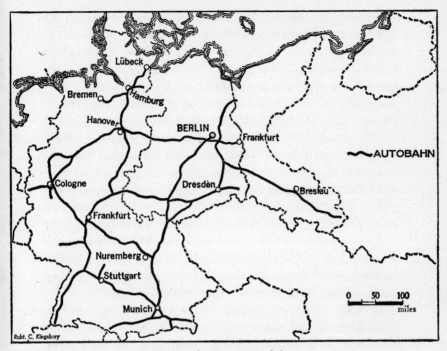

Fig. 13. The German Autobahnen

This condition was to some extent remedied when in the 1930s the programme was begun of building super-highways or *Autobahnen*. The whole road system was severely damaged during the war. The road surface deteriorated everywhere, and bridges were destroyed. In the Bizone alone, it was claimed, 8,100 kilometres of main road were made impassable and 4,808 bridges were destroyed. By the early 1950s these had all been repaired, and the system of *Autobahnen* was being extended. It is planned to cover the Federal Republic with a broad pattern of these super-highways. The map (Figure 13) shows the roads built, under construction, and planned. It is implicit in this map that access to the chief ports is a major consideration, and that the link between South and North Germany—which means also between Switzerland and Scandinavia—is particularly important. Within a short time it may be possible to drive on these super-highways between all the more important cities of the Federal Republic.

These roads are intensively used. Nothing demonstrates better the material prosperity of modern Germany than the processions of slow-moving diesel trucks as they make their way along the *Autobahnen* and turn off at the well-spaced intersections to reach the small industrial towns *en route*; this is in striking contrast to the emptiness of the *Autobahnen* in the Soviet-occupied Zone. The number of lorries has increased rapidly in the last ten years, but this rate of increase has been more than equalled by the rate of increase of the private car. Hitler talked about the small 'people's car', which his government planned to build in vast numbers. It has fallen to the Federal Republic to implement this boast. The Volkswagen is far from being the only small car, and it now has many rivals on the roads. The number of private cars has risen from about half a million in 1950 to over four millions in 1960.

In West Germany, as also in the United Kingdom, the United States and many other countries, road transport by lorry and car is becoming a serious threat to the older forms of transport. The flexibility of road transport, the ability of road vehicles to go from door to door, gives it advantages over both rail and water. Many of the factories engaged in light industries rely almost wholly on road transport for the delivery of raw materials and the distribution of manufactured goods.

Now the pipeline constitutes in some degree a threat to all the older forms of transport. It has long been the only convenient means of moving gas. It is now beginning to replace the river-barge, and with the completion of the proposed system of pipelines all the crude oil will move by pipeline from the ports to refineries scattered through Germany.

Foreign Trade

In a period of a dozen years the Federal Republic of Germany has transformed itself into one of the foremost commercial nations in the world. The expansion of industrial production has been accompanied by a growth in exports, so rapid and successful as to become almost embarrassing. Year after year the total value of German exports has exceeded that of imports, and, after making allowances for a considerable expenditure by Germany for commercial, transport, and other services, the balance of payments has been consistently favourable. Indeed, the Federal Government has at times been obliged to stimulate imports, because so heavy an export balance was having the effect of accumulating in German hands embarrassingly large holdings of foreign currencies and increasing the danger of inflation.

The pattern of Germany's foreign trade is a normal one for a densely populated and highly industrialized country. Imports are dominated by foodstuffs, industrial raw materials, and certain highly specialized factory products. German agriculture has been, as we have seen, relatively highly protected. Bread grains and fodder have dominated the imported foods, but have been subjected to certain quota restrictions. Wheat is the most important, and the increasing volume of import in recent years has reflected the consumers' trend away from coarse grains. Imports of coffee, cocoa, oil-seeds, and citrus and tropical fruits have also increased sharply, again emphasizing the improving living standards within Germany. It is to be assumed that this trend will continue as long as the country enjoys its present level of prosperity.

Industrial raw materials make up over a third of total imports by value. All the raw cotton, natural rubber, and vegetable oils and tropical fibres consumed have to be imported. A considerable proportion of the metalliferous ores, including about half of the iron ore, have to be obtained outside the country. About two-thirds of the petroleum is imported, as well as important quantities of wool, skins, hides, and lumber. Along with the raw materials a large and growing amount of semi-manufactured goods is also imported. The German trade classification includes spun textile yarn, sawn lumber, refined oil, and smelted or concentrated metalliferous ores, in this category.

In some instances the materials have undergone relatively little processing and most become the raw materials of German manufacturing industries.

Manufactured goods constitute the most varied, and in recent years also the largest category of German imports. It is a characteristic of the more developed manufacturing countries that they do a very large amount of business with one another. Germany's table of imports includes textiles, chemicals, and the products of the electrical and engineering industries. There is nothing unusual or illogical in this. Many of the requirements of a modern industrialized society are so varied and so specialized that it is cheaper for each of these countries to specialize in the manufacture of some only of these items, relying upon trade with the others to supply the rest of its needs. This has come to be the accepted pattern. It explains why the Federal Republic, in spite of possessing a developed and efficient engineering industry, nevertheless imports certain types of electrical, textile, and office machinery, and purchases abroad certain pharmaceutical goods despite its own immense chemical industry.

Thus goods which are fully manufactured or substantially so, make up no less than about 31 per cent of Germany's import trade. The range and variety of these goods is likely to increase, as demand broadens and becomes more sophisticated. The following table shows the breakdown of German imports into these three categories during the past ten years:

	1952	1954	1959	1960
Foodstuffs	6,064·7	7,151·0	10,730·7	11,245·8
Raw materials	}7,992·4	8,977·8	{7,748·8	9,268·5
Semi-manufactures			{5,976·5	8,061·1
Manufactured goods	2,145·8	3,208·3	11,029·8	13,746·1
	16,202·9	19,337·1	35,485·8	42,323·5

(in millions of D-Marks)

Germany's export trade shows a similar range and variety. The export trade has been helped by the formerly low costs of production in Germany and also by the re-equipment and rationalization of industrial plant. The following table shows the rapidly mounting volume of the export trade:

1950	8,362	1956	30,861
1951	14,577	1957	35,968
1952	16,909	1958	36,998
1953	18,526	1959	41,184
1954	22,035	1960	47,964
1955	25,717		

(millions of D-Marks)

Within this expanding volume of trade manufactured goods have constituted an increasing percentage. Germany is not a significant exporter of foodstuffs. Wines and delicacies and other foodstuffs, however significant they may appear in the shops in Great Britain and America, made up only 2·3 per cent of total exports in 1960. Nor are raw materials at present of great importance in Germany's export trade. Coal and coke made up about 80 per cent of the total value of German exports in early post-war years. German coal was in such great demand in neighbouring states that a system of export quotas was established. In the early 1950s the European coal shortage eased, and German exports of coal and coal products declined both in the aggregate and, even more sharply, as a percentage of total exports. At the same time manufactured goods and, in particular, the products of the engineering and related industries have grown. They now make up about 82 per cent of Germany's exports. Within this general group, automobiles retain the pride of place which they have occupied for some seven years. The Volkswagen has become one of the widest selling of small cars, and the Mercedes Benz, among more highly priced vehicles. The export trade in precision instruments, photographic equipment, and electrical machinery has regained its pre-war importance. Shipbuilding has developed as an export industry, and contracts for large-scale steel construction, such as the building of bridges, dams, and steelworks, are responsible for the export of large quantities of equipment. The

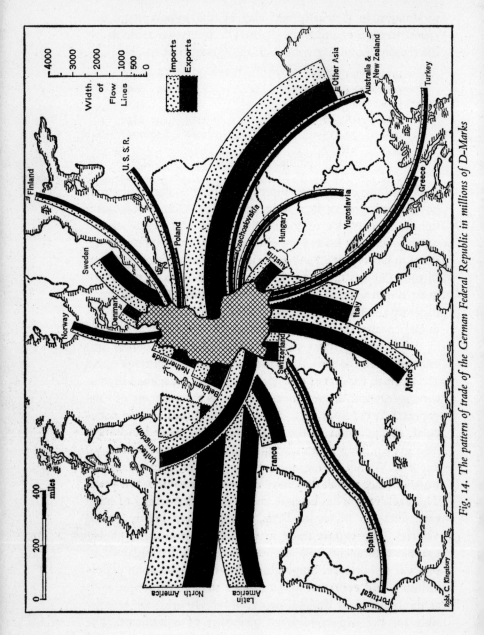

Fig. 14. The pattern of trade of the German Federal Republic in millions of D-Marks

following table shows the main categories of exports from the
Federal Republic in 1960:

	million DM	%
Foodstuffs	1,091	2·4
Raw materials	2,182	4·6
Semi-manufactures	5,007	10·5
Manufactured goods	39,506	82·5
	47,786	100

The geographical spread of Germany's foreign trade presents
some interesting problems. In few of her trading partners is
there even an approximate equality between the value of
German exports and imports. In general, it may be said that,
in her commercial relations with the industrial countries of
Western Europe, Germany sells more than she buys. In her
dealings with the primary producers, which supply the wool
and cotton, cocoa, coffee, and vegetable oils, Germany purchases more than she is able to pay for by exports. She is thus
obliged to rely on the currencies which she obtains from her
heavy sales to such countries as Belgium, Norway, Switzerland, and Austria to pay for her excess purchases in, for
example, the United States and the African and Middle Eastern
countries. The resulting pattern of trade is illustrated in Figure 14.
The key to Germany's trade is her export of factory products,
primarily to her industrial neighbours in Western Europe. This
trade is bound up with the question of her political relations
with them and with their common membership in the European Common Market. These politico-economic relations
between Germany and her neighbours will occupy our last
chapter.

6

Germany and Europe

The military defeat of Germany in 1945 and the occupation of its territory by the armies of Great Britain, France, the United States, and the Soviet Union removed from the European scene, at least temporarily, a force of the greatest political and economic importance. For a time there was neither a German government nor a German state. These have been re-established partly because they had to be—Europe could not tolerate a political vacuum in its midst—and partly because the self-interest of Germany's neighbours required that, in some shape or other, Germany be re-created.

In its simplest terms the problem was this. Europe—or at least Western Europe—feared a revival of German militarism and a renewed threat to its security. At the same time, Western Europe depended on the products of German industry to satisfy part of its own peace-time wants. These two concerns involved the Western Allies in contradictions and changes of policy. The steel industry, considered to be a primary source of military strength, was restricted and partially dismantled; the coal-mining industry, on the other hand, was given every encouragement to expand, because coal was in short supply in the neighbouring states. The political fear that Germany would again become a potentially strong military power was out-weighed by the economic need to rebuild German industry and to satisfy the needs of a Europe desperately short of fuel, of food, and of consumers' goods. This problem had arisen before; J. M. Keynes had examined it in 1919, and had then come to the conclusion that Europe needed Germany. 'Round Germany as a central support', he wrote, 'the rest of the

European economic system grouped itself, and on the prosperity and enterprise of Germany the prosperity of the rest of the Continent mainly depended. The increasing pace of Germany gave her neighbours an outlet for their products, in exchange for which the enterprise of the German merchant supplied them with their chief requirements at a low price.'* This related to the Europe of the years before the First World War. The pattern of economic relationships has changed greatly since then. But J. M. Keynes's conclusion, that 'the statistics of the economic interdependence of Germany and her neighbours are overwhelming' remained true of the period between the First and the Second World Wars, and has again become true of the present situation.

We thus have, in a sense, the political fears of Germany's neighbours in conflict with their economic needs and desires. The long, inept discussion of dismantling and levels of industry illuminates this dichotomy. The Treaty of Dunkirk, of March 1947, with its repeated emphasis on the dangers of renewed German aggression, shows political considerations still triumphing over economic. The Treaty of Brussels, signed exactly a year later by France, the Benelux group, and the United Kingdom, revealed a change of emphasis. It called for collaboration in economic and social matters; it did not mention Germany by name, and, by implication, it left room for Germany to accede to the treaty itself.

The contrast in spirit between the two treaties, only a year apart in time, is considerable. It would be easy to explain it in terms of a triumph of economic good sense over political fears and prejudices. In fact, however, the change came about in the spring of 1947, when the Moscow Conference on Germany broke up, and the Cold War, which had, perhaps, been implicit in events for almost two years, now became a matter of public record. The balance of Europe had become disturbed, and a new Germany was slowly and reluctantly being called into existence to redress that balance. A political, as distinct from an

* J. M. Keynes, *The Economic Consequences of Peace*, London, 1919, p. 14.

economic need for Germany was shaping up in Western Europe. It is impossible to separate completely the political and the economic aspects of the relations to Germany of her neighbours, both western and eastern. They are indissolubly linked. Economic concessions are made in return for political accommodations, and vice versa. Nevertheless, for purposes of narration it is desirable to pull them apart as fully as is possible.

Political Relations of the Federal Republic of Germany

The Western political attitude to Germany was simple. It sprang from the fear of a re-armed and sovereign Germany, and its positive policy was at first to limit Germany's political power and military potential. This objective was, of course, qualified in different ways in each of the West European states, and in all of them its sharpness was modified in some degree by economic considerations. In France the fear of Germany was openly expressed. France gave way with considerable reluctance on the policy of economic fusion of the three western zones of Germany. At each step forward towards German political sovereignty, it was France which applied the brake most strongly, and it was France which shied away from re-arming Germany, thus wrecking the European Defence Community in 1954. Nevertheless, the three occupation zones of West Germany were economically and politically merged; controls were gradually withdrawn; the rights of occupation forces were clearly limited and defined by the Occupation Statute, and in 1955 the Federal Republic of Germany was recognized as sovereign by those states which had previously joined in controlling and occupying it.

Already West Germany had become a political ally of its Western neighbours. In April 1949 the rather formless Brussels Pact had been effectively replaced by a treaty establishing the North Atlantic Treaty Organization (NATO). The parties to the Treaty, which included all the western neighbours of the Federal Republic except Switzerland and Austria, but excluded the Federal Republic itself, undertook 'to eliminate conflict in their international economic policies and (to) encourage economic collaboration between any or all of them', and 'separately and jointly, by means of continuous and effective self-help and mutual aid', to 'maintain and develop their individual and collective capacity to resist armed attack'. Lastly, the parties to the Treaty agreed 'that an armed attack against one or more of them in Europe or North America shall be considered an attack against them all'. In October 1954 the Federal Government was invited to accede to the North Atlantic Treaty. The invitation was accepted, and membership became effective on May 9, 1955, four days after the rebirth of sovereignty of the Federal Republic of Germany.

Thus the political fears that had been expressed by France and her Western Allies, and the political controls which they had sought to exercise had evaporated within ten years of the end of the war. They had, in fact, lasted a shorter period of time, despite the unconditional surrender of Germany in May 1945, than the similar political controls imposed by the Treaty of Versailles in 1919. West Germany, as a sovereign state, can adopt whatever limits she may choose on her industry; she can influence the direction of her trade and the structure of her economy entirely at her own discretion. Economic associations and agreements to which the Federal Government is a party are now freely entered into, and are a product of negotiation between it and the authorities of other states. Such actions must be held to reflect the self-interest of West Germany; it is interesting that many of them seem also to be in the best interests of the wider European community.

Economic Relations of the Federal Republic of Germany

The North Atlantic Treaty of 1949 had placed military and political collaboration ahead of economic. Already West Germany had been included in the scope of the Marshall Plan through its representation by the three occupying Powers. In 1949 the Federal Government itself began to participate in the negotiations of the Organization for European Economic

Co-operation (OEEC), which existed to implement the Marshall Plan for Europe. Up to this point the objectives of policy had been the re-establishing of the level of prosperity, and the pattern of interdependence and exchange that had existed before the war. In May 1950 a big step forward was proposed by Robert Schuman, the French Foreign Minister, which would have the effect, if implemented, of carrying European integration far beyond the dreams of pre-war years. He proposed the creation of a common market in the raw materials and the half-finished products of the iron and steel industries. These included coal and coke, iron ore and metal scrap, cast iron and steel 'semis'. The background to Schuman's proposal was provided by two quite different considerations.

The first of these had been summarized in a report, *European Steel Trends in the Setting of the World Market*, which the United Nations Economic Commission for Europe had published during the previous year. This report argued that steel-making capacity was being expanded so rapidly in the world as a whole that there was grave danger of total capacity far exceeding the expected demand. In these conditions the report, which was directed to the European industry, recommended 'a genuine specialization of production on a regional basis with a view to enabling producers to carry out co-ordinated production pro- grammes to ensure optimum efficiency', and, in order to implement this, 'steps to ensure the free movement from one specialized region to another of the various types of flat products thus produced'. Schuman's proposal actually went further than this, including all that contributes not merely to flat products but to all the other forms assumed by iron and steel goods. His recommendations were hailed as an important step towards securing both the prosperity of the West Euro- pean steel industry and also the closer integration of the European Community. But the noblest of political gestures are grounded in national self-interest. France stood to benefit as much as Europe from the acceptance of the Schuman Plan.

France had been particularly fearful of two aspects of Germany: the military and the industrial. At this date there was no German army; the country was under military occupation, and, for a time at least, France had nothing to fear from this source. Heavy industry was regarded as the handmaid of militarism. But to explain militarism in terms of the steel industry is, of course, to explain nothing. This view springs to some extent from a widespread pacifist fallacy that the danger of war arose from the arms race, and not vice versa. Whatever the source of the misconception, the French leaders and many others were convinced that if the German coal, iron, and steel industries could be placed under some international authority, however limited its power, one more element would have been removed from Germany's desire and capacity to wage war.

A second element in the French position was her own shortage of materials during the critical post-war years. France has, in Lorraine, the largest reserve of iron ore in Europe, and her own iron and steel industry is based upon this resource. France's resources in fuel are, however, by no means commensurate with those in iron ore. Her not inconsiderable reserves were notably deficient in coal of coking quality. To some extent this shortage can be offset by blending and beneficiating local coal, but France remained heavily dependent upon German coal from the Ruhr. Destruction and dislocation had reduced the supply of German coal, and the exportable surplus had to be allocated to users on a quota basis by the Allied Coal Commission. France was unable to get all the coal she needed—but neither could any other state. In France, however, there was a suspicion that the Germans were in some way defaulting on what France considered to be their obligations, and the kind of suspicion that had led to the occupation of the Ruhr in 1923 carried over into the years following the Second World War. If, under the cover of some such international organization as Schuman was proposing, it became technically and legally impossible for Germany to withhold coal needed by France or by any other consumer, or to discriminate in its fuel deliveries against any state, then the position of the French iron and steel industries would, it was supposed, be that much the more secure.

The fact that motives were mixed must not be allowed to detract from the essential bigness of Schuman's proposal. It was the first move, if we omit the formation of Benelux, in the creation of a functional unity in Western Europe. If the Schuman Plan had not been tried out for a restricted range of commodities, and if it had not proved to be completely successful, there could now be no European Economic Community.

The Treaty which established the European Coal and Steel Community came into effect in 1952, after its ratification by the member states: France, the Federal Republic of Germany, Italy, and the Benelux group. Customs duties, restrictions, and discriminatory rates were gradually abolished. It ceased to be possible for any member state to attract any branch of the coal, iron, and steel industries to its borders by political means, nor did any industrial location have any advantage that was not implicit in the cost of labour, materials, and freight. Industrial concerns, looking for a site for a new plant, were encouraged to choose within the whole area of the community, confident that governments could not influence their choice by political means.

The result has been to extinguish inefficient units of production, which had hitherto been kept in production by some kind of governmental support, and to lower the price, relative to other commodities, of iron and steel products. Despite the predictions of 1949 that steel capacity would soon be excessive for certain ranges of production, European and foreign demand continued to increase, and in 1960 production of steel from the six member states was more than twice what it had been before the Second World War.

The creation of the European Coal and Steel Community focused attention again on two contentious areas, which had done much to disrupt Franco-German relations: the Saarland and the river Mosel. The Saar coalfield is not among the larger and more important in Europe, and the qualities of coal which it produces have a very limited usefulness. In 1919 France gained, by the terms of the Treaty of Versailles, the right to operate the mines for a period of fifteen years, after which a plebiscite was to determine the future of the area. Reasons for this were mixed. France put forward certain historical claims to the area, based upon their occupation by the French during the Revolutionary wars. The reason for the acquiescence of Great Britain and the United States in this action was France's need for coal until such time as her own damaged mines in Nord and Pas-de-Calais could be restored to production. The same kind of confused reasoning influenced the French after 1945. The Saarland, which reverted to Germany after the plebiscite of 1935, lay in the French zone of occupation. The French established a separate government for the territory, brought it into close economic relations with France, and allowed the Saarlanders a more favourable food ration than the rest of the French Zone was accorded. For a time the French pursued a policy of detaching the Saarland from Germany. Then growing prosperity in Germany itself made the French connection less attractive. The historical association of France with the Saarland never had much significance. If there had ever been any justification for the French absorption of the Saarland, it lay in France's need for the fuel of the Saar coalfield. At a blow this reason was destroyed by the creation of the Coal and Steel Community, for France now had free access to the coal of the Ruhr. By an agreement of October 1956 France undertook to return the Saarland to Germany on January 1, 1957. By the summer of 1959 the territory was integrated into the economy of the Federal Republic of Germany, though it has not fully severed its connection with France. France is obliged by the Saar Statute to take a certain quantity of Saar coal, and certain French products enjoy duty-free entry into the Saarland.

A second shadow had been cast over the relations between France and Germany by the question of using the river Mosel to transport coal and iron ore between Lorraine and the Rhineland. Nothing, it would appear from the map, could be more conducive to the development and prosperity of the iron and steel industries in both Lorraine and the Ruhr than the existence of the rivers which join them. We have already seen (p. 102) that while the Rhine is naturally navigable, the Mosel is not fit for use by large barges without extensive dredging and deepening. Proposals to improve its physical conditions had been made soon after the adoption of the basic process of steel-making, patented in 1879, had revolutionized the importance of the Lorraine ores. The most difficult sections of the river lay in Germany, and it was on the opposition of German vested interests that the proposals to canalize or regulate the river had foundered. Broadly, it was supposed that the creation of the cheaper means of river transport would confer greater advantages on Lorraine industrialists than on those of the Lower Rhineland. The effect of the Coal and Steel Community has been to subtract national rivalries from the competitive positions of the several iron and steel industries. It is no longer a question—if, in fact, it ever was—of Lorraine's gain being the Ruhr's loss. Anything that facilitates and cheapens steel production anywhere in Europe can be regarded as beneficial to the Western European community as a whole. German resistance to the scheme to canalize the Mosel was abandoned in return for France's agreement to allow the Saarland to be re-incorporated into Germany if it wished. The Federal Government undertook to facilitate the construction of locks and other works on the river. Preliminary survey work has already been completed and the actual work of regulating the river is now nearing completion.

Germany and the Common Market

The treaty which created the Coal and Steel Community envisaged the extension of its scope to cover all articles of trade: agricultural products, industrial raw materials, and manufactured goods. In 1955 the Foreign Ministers of the six members of the Community met at Messina and worked out a plan for a common market. The treaty which embodied the final proposals was signed at Rome in March 1957. It came into effect on January 1, 1958, and the first steps were taken in the progressive reduction of tariffs between the Six, and in the levelling up or down of the tariff barrier *around* them were taken on January 1, 1959. The process of tariff reduction has made considerable progress, and has even been accelerated beyond the speed envisaged by the original agreement. Its objects reach further than the creation of a common market; they extend to the alignment of 'the economic policies of its members with a view to promoting economic growth and stability and strengthening relations among its members'.* Its role is not merely permissive; it includes positive action to secure prosperity and expansion.

How then does the Federal German Government fit into the commercial and economic pattern presented by the Six? This question raises the important and, in some degree, conflicting problems of German agriculture and the German export of industrial products. In many countries of Western Europe agricultural practice is relatively inefficient and in most it enjoys some degree of protection. Only in Denmark and the Netherlands does the domestic cost of agricultural production approximate at all closely to the world price of farm commodities. In Germany it is considerably higher, and the farmers are heavily protected. Under existing conditions there is no question that, in the absence of import restrictions, certain of the agricultural products of most other members of the Six could undersell the German farmer in the German market. The treatment of farm products was a critical issue in the discussions which led to the formation of the Economic Community. It would clearly be unrealistic to exclude agricultural products from the operation of the common market, and impossible to abolish quota and tariff restrictions suddenly and without preparing the farming

* Emile Benoit, *Europe at Sixes and Sevens*, Columbia University Press, 1961, p. 4.

community for it. For this reason, agricultural goods were exempted from the first round of tariff reductions, and the enlargement of import quotas is due to proceed much more slowly in this sector than in all others. Germany thus has a period of a few years in which to prepare for the cold breath of Italian, French, and Dutch competition in agricultural goods. The admission of the United Kingdom, and also Denmark, Norway and perhaps other countries, cannot now be regarded as anything more than a long-term possibility. The United Kingdom would pose no threat to German agriculture; but not so Denmark and Norway, whose agriculture is both specialized and highly efficient.

The structure of German agriculture has, however, been changing rapidly. The number of very small holdings continues to diminish and that of medium-sized to increase; the consolidation of peasant holdings is making progress; the land quality is being improved by draining and the greater use of fertilizer; and both farming itself and the processing of farm produce are becoming more mechanized. At the same time, the present trend in consumption is towards a greater demand for milk, butter, eggs, and meat. This brings with it a gradual shift from bread crops and potatoes towards fodder crops and a greater emphasis on animal husbandry. In these ways the competitive position of the German farmer may be expected to improve to the point where he can meet the challenge of his neighbours without the aid of tariffs and quotas. In the meanwhile he continues in various ways to be subsidized and supported by the Federal Government.

In all other respects the Federal Republic of Germany stands to gain from membership of the European Economic Community. Her ability to import raw materials is largely dependent on sales to her industrialized neighbours, with most of which she has an export surplus. Of her twelve largest export markets, all except the United States are in Western Europe, and they include all of Germany's fellow members of the Economic Community. German exports to her European neighbours consist mainly of manufactured goods. The liberalizing of trade within the Community is likely to result in an increase of imports of manufactured goods into Germany, but it is probable that the total volume of trade will increase and that the Federal Republic will further strengthen its commercial position within the Economic Community as a result of freer trade.

Eastern Europe and the Balkans was once considered an almost exclusively German trading area. German capital was invested there; the agricultural surpluses of these areas was exchanged for German factory products. This eastward orientation of German trade seemed so natural that it required no explanation. But it received its final, as it certainly received its clearest, expression in the commercial treaties negotiated in the 1930s with the East European countries by Hjalmar Schacht. Now this association is broken, except for the East European trade carried on by the so-called 'German Democratic Republic' (the Soviet Zone of Germany). Only 2 per cent of the total foreign trade of the Federal Republic of Germany is with the East European satellites of the Soviet Union. No less than 62 per cent, in 1960, was with non-Communist Europe. The change in the orientation of Germany's trade is, like its denser population and higher degree of industrialization, another of the characteristics which distinguish the new Germany that has arisen, both literally and metaphorically, from the ashes of the old.

The question of the changed economic orientation of West Germany at once raises another: that of the incorporation of the Soviet-occupied Zone into the economy of the Soviet *bloc*. The volume of trade between the two major fragments of the former German Reich is small, and is at present made up mainly of fuel and other unprocessed materials. Most of the foreign trade of the Federal Republic and the Soviet Zone is with the allies of each lying respectively to west and east.

Economic development within the Soviet-held Zone has been by a series of development plans, each integrated with

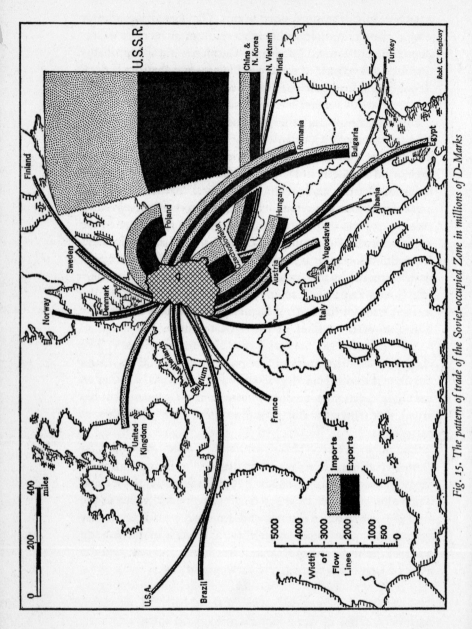

Fig. 15. The pattern of trade of the Soviet-occupied Zone in millions of D-Marks

those of its Communist neighbours. Within the Communist *bloc* a considerable degree of national specialization has been achieved. The Zone continues to specialize in those branches of industry for which it is already well equipped: chemicals, precision engineering, and with such goods it supplies part of the needs of its Communist neighbours.

On the other hand, new industries, such as a great extension of iron and steel production, have been established in order to compensate for the loss of West German sources of materials. The Soviet Zone is obliged to depend for the supply of raw materials and certain types of fuel on the Communist *bloc*. The new blast furnaces are supplied with iron ore from Krivoi Rog, in the Ukraine, and with fuel from Poland and the Soviet Union. Petroleum is supplied by pipeline from the Caucasus or the Urals. The Soviet-occupied Zone has come to depend on the Soviet Union for the supply of a wide range of materials —raw materials as well as manufactured. And this dependence is likely to continue, as industry in the Zone comes to be adjusted in its technology to Soviet sources of supply.

The commercial and economic ties between the Federal Republic and its western allies on the one hand, and those between the Soviet-occupied Zone and the rest of the Communist *bloc* on the other hand, have grown more intimate with the passage of time. A change in political outlook can occur quickly, and can be reversed at short notice. A change in economic orientation and dependence, on the other hand, is bound to take place slowly. It is dependent upon adjustments in technology, but once achieved can be altered or given a new orientation only with singular difficulty. In this sense, the economic division of Germany and of Europe is more fundamental, less susceptible of sudden or rapid change than the political. For the foreseeable future the German Federal Republic has become the economic ally of Western Europe. The Soviet-occupied Zone and the lands beyond the Oder and Neisse will similarly continue to reinforce with their resources and industry the power of the Communist *bloc*.

Index